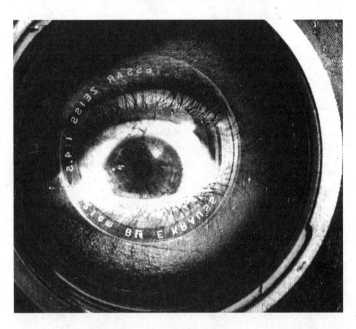

GRANTA 62, SUMMER 1998

EDITOR   Ian Jack
DEPUTY EDITOR   Robert Winder
MANAGING EDITOR   Karen Whitfield
EDITORIAL ASSISTANT   Sophie Harrison

FINANCE   Geoffrey Gordon
ASSOCIATE PUBLISHER   Sally Lewis
SALES   David Hooper
PUBLICITY   Gail Lynch, Rebecca Linsley
SUBSCRIPTIONS   John Kirkby, Mark Williams
TO ADVERTISE CONTACT   Jenny Shramenko 0171 704 9776

PUBLISHER   Rea S. Hederman

Granta, 2-3 Hanover Yard, Noel Road, London N1 8BE
Tel 0171 704 9776 Fax 0171 704 0474
e-mail for editorial: editorial@grantamag.co.uk

Granta USA LLC, 1755 Broadway, 5th Floor, New York, NY 10019-3780, USA
Website: www.granta.com

TO SUBSCRIBE call 0171 704 0470 or e-mail: subs@grantamag.co.uk.
A one-year subscription (four issues) costs £24.95 (UK), £32.95 (rest of Europe) and
£39.95 (rest of the world).

Granta is printed in the United States of America. The paper used in this publication meets the
minimum requirements of American National Standard for Information Sciences—Permanence of
Paper for Printed Library Materials, ANSI Z39.48-1984. ♾

Granta is published by Granta Publications and distributed in the United Kingdom by Bloomsbury,
38 Soho Square, London W1V 5DF; and is published in the United States by Granta USA LLC, and
distributed by Penguin Books USA Inc, 375 Hudson Street, New York, NY 10014, USA and in
Canada by Penguin Books Canada Ltd, 10 Alcorn Avenue, Toronto, Ontario, Canada M4V 3B2. This
selection copyright © 1998 Granta Publications.

Design: The Senate
Front cover photograph: A young Dayak man early this century by Charles Hose,
Royal Anthropological Institute
Back cover: Niall McInerney

ISBN 0 903141 18 3

GRANTA 62

What young men do

Royal Festival Hall
Queen Elizabeth Hall
Purcell Room

Literature Events
June Highlights:

Hanif Kureishi, Greek Poetry and Fiction, **Lemn Sissay** and South African Performance Poets, **C K Williams**, **Windrush Day** celebrating the literary life of the first generation of Caribbeans to arrive in Britain in 1948 including **George Lamming**, **Beryl Gilroy** and **Caryl Phillips**.

July Highlights:

Peruvian tales from **Nicholas Shakespeare**, Women on the Road - **Emily Perkins**, **Jill Dawson**, **Margo Daly** & **Kathy Page**, John Heath-Stubbs' 80th Birthday, **John Ashbery** and **Jorie Graham**.

Hayward Gallery
on the South Bank • London

Exhibitions

ANISH KAPOOR
30 April - 14 June

BRUCE NAUMAN
16 July - 6 September

ADDRESSING THE CENTURY:
100 YEARS OF ART & FASHION
8 October - 11 January

BOX OFFICE **0171 960 4242** quote GRA when booking
BROCHURE LINE **0171 921 0734** (Literature or Exhibitions Bulletins)
OR SURF **www.sbc.org.uk**

sbc

INTRODUCTION

A word which should frighten more people, certainly more editors, than it does is: relaunch. Together with 'relabel', 'repackage' and 'rebrand', it smacks of marketing tradecraft, diligent attention to focus groups, flipcharts and that ritual called 'the presentation' which is conducted by young men from advertising agencies, who, tieless, crop-headed and sermonizing, might easily be priests. They speak the vocabulary sacred to modern capitalism—'brand identity', 'core values', 'market share'—and lo, if you accept their sacraments, 'the product' is born again: which is to say that it looks dramatically different to convey a change of substance, though substantially it may remain the same. Sometimes this process seems to work—see the British Labour Party's electoral victory in 1997, though there it was also allied to a fundamental political shift—but often it fails to rectify the desperation which first summoned it. Old wine in new bottles, mutton dressed as lamb: these are ancient epigrams which indicate long-term public resistance to the vanities and fancies of corporations, and editors.

So: *Granta* has not been relaunched. It simply looks a little different. *Granta*'s old design served it well for nearly twenty years; the changes to its minimalism are mainly to make the magazine's intention clearer (minimalism can sometimes be opaque). The typeface for titles and text is Sabon rather than Times; there is also the sparse use of a sans-serif face, Bell Gothic, and a few adjustments to the cover, where the rubric 'The Magazine of New Writing' has been moved from the back to the front. I have to admit that I'm often troubled by this definition. 'New Writing' suggests, at least in Britain, state subsidy and difficult, possibly unpleasurable, literary experimentation, writing mainly of concern to the person who has written it. Also, it omits new photography, which *Granta* also publishes. Also, as any marketeer would say, it is a producerist rather than a consumerist tag (why not 'The Magazine of New Reading'?). Also, there is the dangerous possibility of misidentification with New Labour. But there is no way out. New writing is what *Granta* exists to publish, in the belief that writing, especially if it is fresh and original, still offers the most interesting, and the most telling, reflection of ourselves and the world.

Two parlous states receive intimate examination in this issue: the first is marriage, the second Indonesia.   **IJ**

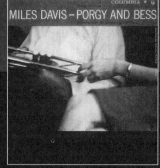
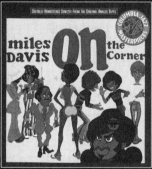
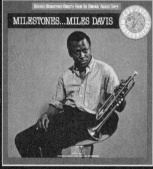

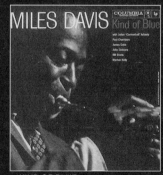

THE SEPARATED
Tim Lott

January

It is a short January day, unseasonably warm. The afternoon is getting dark and it isn't yet four o'clock. The house is a three storey, a family house.

On the top floor: two bedrooms, slumber, awakenings from dreams, small excitements becoming sadnesses.

On the middle floor: a sitting room, with a third bedroom behind, this time strewn for play. There are children's paintings, colourful messes on the walls, toys. The children, sisters, one four and one two years old, are absent on a visit to their grandmother.

On the ground floor: the guts of the house. A whitewashed bathroom, evacuations, submersions, the faint scrape of razors across a leg or a face. Behind the bathroom, a small concrete yard where a cigarette is sometimes taken, out of sight of the children. You can sit on the blue plastic sandpit, moulded in the shape of a clam. Inside, the main room on this floor has a flat-pack kitchen, carelessly assembled, varnished gappy floorboards, a sofa made grubby with the food the children spill. There is a table in the style of a Fifties diner at the front, filling the curved space in the bay window. It is a basic metropolitan home, not luxurious, a little dirty.

The couple inside have just returned from a day at the winter sales. The man is on the short side, losing hair, his face wearing a bloom of frustration. The woman is dark-haired, Mediterranean, almost too slender. Pretty, appearing in any light far younger than she actually is. Her face is pale—always avoiding the sun—and her body is quite still.

There are seven or eight moths floating in the room. They made a nest here three months ago, and will not be discouraged by the remedial sprigs of lavender that are carefully placed on mantels, fireplaces and window frames. The moths move too slowly. You can easily catch one in your hand and destroy it with the tiniest movement. The man does this now, with an infant's sense of satisfied cruelty.

The couple are squared-up to each other, about five feet apart. The man is speaking loudly and purposefully. He knows exactly what he is saying and that perhaps he shouldn't be saying it, but he can't find the will or interest to prevent himself.

Words are now in the air, like the moths. Or not so much like moths, but small black birds.

'I fucking hate you. You fucking cunt.'

His unintended mission completed, the man walks out of the room. The words are still reverberating in his head. He leaves in order to calm himself. He knows he has gone much further than he has ever been in such a transaction between himself and his wife of six— is that right?—yes, six years. Six and a half, he thinks. He feels himself strangely excited by the freedom of the moment, while simultaneously shamed. The words have crossed several long-established borders that have previously contained their arguments. It is as far away as they have been from the starting line, or some imagined zone of healing and reconciliation. The man has never struck his wife, but imagines that this is how it must feel. He is shocked that it feels this pure, that it feels this real.

Five, maybe ten minutes have passed. He has been pacing the first-floor front room, tripping over, then cursing, stray dolls, cute dinosaurs, a battery-powered tyrannosaurus with soft teeth and a single eye. He gathers himself, and starts the journey down the stairs. This is difficult. He knows the space he has left will be transformed in some way he does not yet understand. He doesn't know what he is going to say.

His wife doesn't seem to have moved from where he left her. She is waiting for a resolution of some kind. Her mouth is set in an unmoving, crimson line. The man has to go and pick up the children in a few minutes. Things cannot be left as they are.

The man's voice is vibrating perceptibly when he speaks. He had only imagined that he had calmed down. The man says:

'I just want to say one thing.'

He looks at her face for the first time. It is blank.

'I'm calm now. And settled. And I just want to say. I want you to know that...'

He imagines that she is expecting him to apologize. He hopes so, so that she will be caught on the wrong foot.

'I want you to know that I meant every word that I just said. So wake up and smell the fucking coffee—before it's too late.'

And with this, he makes to leave with what he hopes to be a flourish. He likes the sound of his last sentence. It is an expression his younger brother uses, and he has borrowed it for this purpose. But his wife remains neutral, and rather than looking shocked or annoyed, looks perplexed. She says, in a voice he has heard so much, so often, it has become, for the most part, inaudible:

'What does that mean?'

The man is irritated that the flow of his exit has been interrupted.

'What does what mean?'

'*Wake up and smell the coffee.* What does that *mean?* I don't understand.'

It's a phrase she has never heard before, and in the heightened emotion of the moment she's unable to infer its meaning. So then the man has carefully to explain the phrase to her, so that the flourish with which he hoped to leave the house is deflated into lameness. He shakes his head in disgust and astonishment—not at his wife, now, but at invisible half-imagined gods. For even now, in the heat and heart of collapse, in the furnace of his temporary hate—strictly temporary, for he likes his wife often enough, well enough—they still can't understand each other. That his simple threat and insult, his searing warning, is met again with the endless tattoo that passes between them, publicly, privately, internally, verbally, symbolically, literally.

I don't, I don't, I don't *understand* you.

Exercises in Words

The man is a writer. This is a word he privately savours, always careful to distinguish it, sniffily, defensively, from the description 'journalist', the coin of whose trade, he believes, are mute facts skilfully assembled, opinions racked in a penny store, the minting of smart turns of phrase which are insufficiently true. *Writer.* To use that word accurately about himself he considers to be his greatest achievement, in a life full of garish stumbles, mistakes and small terrors.

He has a certain reputation for writing pieces of a confessional nature, exposing his tenderest parts, like a courting mandrill, for public inspection. Some find this tasteless. So occasionally, he writes about his life as if it were fiction. One or two commentators think that this is simply a stylistic conceit. But this is not, in fact, the case. It is the man's way of taking refuge, a protective coating over what is too raw. It is also a way, he hopes, of sparing himself embarrassment. The fear of embarrassment, he thinks, is one of the world's most underrated forces.

He often wishes that he could turn his life into fiction, or be given the option to claim it as fiction. It's what he does in his head all the time. Laid out like that, it acquires a grace and tidiness that real life lacks. The man's ugly abuse offset by considerations of style, structure and imagined elegance of grammar.

But what he writes is printed in his memory. It happened, though not exactly like that, not just-so, though this is exactly how he remembers it happening. His wife's memories, his children's, will be different.

The couple in his story, the story in his head, are himself and his partner. The 'third person', this godlike perspective, can only do so much to distance him from reality, to grant him absolution. He is Tee, and his wife is Ess. They have been married six years. Six and a half. It has all been coming a long time. Perhaps since that summer day, 1 July 1991, when he kissed her under the bridal veil, feeling, even then, a sense of theatre, of acting.

She was stiff with tension, frozen at the altar.

More Exercises: Again with Words

The man, Tee, considers it vital to the successful execution of his skill that he can see what lies underneath the skin of people. That, at the very least, he can make good guesses. He prides himself on his expertise at communication.

Communication. The man and the woman both know now that things are extreme, stretched dangerously. Tee thinks of a balloon expanding towards a pin. That frail tightness.

Family therapists—so the man and his wife are told—use a well-tested exercise which is designed to *facilitate communication*. These are the words that are used. The man finds it an ugly phrase, with a grain running through it implying homilies and mocked-up concern. Nevertheless, the balloon is about to burst. Unusual remedies, they accept, may be necessary. Both parties—for parties are already how he styles themselves in his mind, as if flexing for formal negotiation— recognize that they need help to find ways over the fences they have erected against understanding each other.

For the man, this fence is made of condescension, an adopted superiority. For the woman it is made of silence, or shouting. Both are expressions of a rearing, kicking anger at something, possibly something deep in the past, that manifests itself perpetually in the present. Or is history, the man wonders, just a way of getting them both off the hook? More and more nowadays, he thinks so.

The exercise, then. The exercise is simple, and, so they are assured, effective. One half of the couple begins a conversation. The other half, instead of answering verbally, writes their reply on a piece of paper, then immediately shows their written answer to the speaker. And thus the conversation progresses. One partner is therefore always silent, their voice converted into text. The couple rotate their roles as speaker and writer, on a daily basis.

The husband and wife gravely try the exercise. Half an hour, four times a week, after the children have gone to bed. A file begins to accumulate of all the arguments that have been eating up the marriage like famished tapeworms. The man stares at a ream of paper, some sides covered in his handwriting—big, intimidating—some sides decorated with hers, smaller, flowing.

He sees scraps of his own scrawled sentences. Only half the conversation, of course, his half. The half which is spoken by Ess is missing, unrecorded, and can only be inferred or remembered.

It's a very hard thing for me to express...somehow it bleeds you dry...your obsessive rituals...do something about what?...of course... but how can I when I don't know its source?...anything else would be asking the impossible...I have to find a way of averting my eyes...how have you done it all your life?...if you can tell me how you can do it, then maybe I'll know how I do it...Not true...! I thought I had accepted your limitations and that you had accepted mine...now it turns out that you don't. Result? War...I don't know.

It comes across as mostly nonsense. Yet reading the scraps is strangely satisfying, sometimes even, he thinks, they read like an oblique poem. In his mind, he calls it 'Sometimes'.

Yes.
Sometimes.
Yes.

Badly.
I don't know.
Why do you think?
The questions are all missing. In life, the other way round. He looks at the other pieces of paper, covered with his wife's handwriting. Now it is his voice that is absent. Perhaps there are some clues here.

Then why are you getting uptight?...you make me feel I should be so grateful...you make me feel guilty. I'm tired...I've always felt it was unfair...I did not say that...what would I be, a housewife, a 'mother'?—NOT ENOUGH. Was that a question, does it require an answer?...OK let's drop it. All I know is that you are different from other fathers...I hate your...stickler for the rules...I'm not a child I don't need boundaries. You can be so rigid sometimes.

He sees a pattern emerging, eventually. Each argument has had a life almost as long as the marriage, repeating, never even mutating much, just kicking along, separately alive, dedicated to its own survival in some obscure way. Seeing those screeds of part-arguments laid out now on paper is salutary. How inescapable those little whorls of ink and dots and lines seemed, how they stretched out and linked like tiny binding tethers.

They are both growing weary of this exercise, which seems less and less like a game, although it has worked in some way, by forcing them to confront the tight patterns that rule their lives. The patterns seem immutable.

A time comes when they have not performed the exercise for several days. Then, one night three days after the man's forty-second birthday, they resume.

A record remains of this night, the record, as it turns out, of the end of their marriage. Sometime later, the man picks up this last scrap of paper and attempts to decode it, to remember the missing questions.

The first answer is:

Pretty bad.

It is written in the hand of Ess, so it is clear that Tee is doing the talking. The question, he remembers clearly, is, 'How are you feeling?'

The next answer is:

I wish I could answer that. We're on different planes—taking different journeys—not meeting anywhere.

The question there is, 'What's the matter?'

He goes on, filling in the gaps as best he can (his wife remembers some questions differently).

Him: *Are you as frightened of this conversation as I am?*

Her: *Yes. Is that why you didn't want to have it?*

Him: *I did want to have it.*

Her: *I hate these 'communications'. It's brought it to a head.*

Him: *I want to ask you one question. It's important that you answer honestly. Do you really really love me, or are you just keeping the marriage afloat because the alternative seems unbearable?*

The man remembers a tiny gap here before she starts writing. She shows him her words on the sheet of paper.

It's the second. But then I also believe(d) you don't love me.

He stares at the paper. Now he feels he knows what she wants. And whether she wants it or not, it's done now.

Well. There's nothing more to say then.

He acknowledges the courage the woman has shown in making her answer. He remembers that they sat there, perfectly still and silent, until the man began to sob, softly at first, then more loudly. The woman reached across to console him...They held each other like that for a short while. For a minute or so, perhaps.

The man had not cried such tears in the marriage—no tears at all, that he can remember—since one day, four or five years previously, when, standing in their kitchen alone, he suddenly stopped his trivial tasks, sat down and began to weep, inexplicably, for some twenty minutes, then resumed his tasks.

This time, though, was different. This time, the cause was all too clear.

The Separated

The man finds this separation an unpredictable experience. Yet it is not the first time it has happened—once before, almost exactly a year ago, they parted, for a matter of six weeks. But this occasion already feels different. No clenching of teeth, or utterances of determination. Just the sense of things now taking their proper course. It feels as if a great weight has been lifted, his interior cleansed by the first batch of deeply shed tears.

That night, the man struggles to unpack a sofa bed on the first floor. The man thinks that he will never share a bed with his wife again, and it does not seem so strange. Perhaps he has been more absent than he has been capable of admitting to himself.

It has been agreed that he will move out of the house in two weeks' time.

He pulls the mechanism of the bed to about a quarter of the way out. It often sticks like this. He wrestles and struggles with it, pulling wildly, nearly toppling the sofa over. It will not come loose. The man becomes enraged; the mechanism has momentarily become his marriage: stiff, stuck, cursed, immovable. Now he attacks it like a glowering enemy, but it remains immobile. The man lets loose a stream of curses, then packs the bed away, and falls on to a single line of sofa cushions, defeated.

He thinks of explosions underground. The system, he thinks, lying there in the darkness, has been building up pressure for so many years, then suddenly a hole appears, then another, then the whole thing blows, and you're soaked, soaked through, and it's dreadful, you might be swept away, but there's an ecstasy in it too.

It is a short-lived feeling. During that first night alone, he hears one of his children crying. He rushes upstairs to see if she wants milk, or if he can cover her with a blanket or bring her a toy. Then halfway up the stairs, he realizes it may not be either of his children, but his wife.

He keeps himself warm against the chill inside him by repeating over and over an incantation.

The present will sink into the past. Everything passes. Things will change. Death and birth and death and birth and death and birth.

He stands looking at his children breathing in their bunk beds. He imagines something here for them has been irretrievably shattered, but that that something may have been a bad thing. Something will be remade. It may be better. He hopes so, but cannot guarantee it.

He fears losing his children. He fears so many things. But at the same time, he feels brave, and far beyond any kind of backslide.

During the next day, the man finds himself beginning idly to calculate the odds—already!—of starting again with someone else, some day, far in the future. There is no one remotely on the horizon. Neither he nor his wife were unfaithful to each other during the marriage, despite occasional flirtations.

What are his chances? He is not young. He is ordinary looking, too stocky. Yet he feels confidence, some sense of power. It is, he realizes, the power of indifference. The strength of loving his children removes other needs. The power of moving himself forward through this situation to the other side makes him feel that choice is within him, no longer buried and latent, but exposed like a vein pulsing in his brow.

He does not do any more crying, except when he tells his younger brother. Then he falls once more into racking sobs. His brother puts his arm round him as if he were the elder, and holds him. When he lets go, Tee is calm.

He tries to convince himself: The children are all right, children are tough.

The last time they split up, the eldest daughter was assailed by asthma, began to suck her thumb, piss herself. On one occasion she smeared shit all over the wall. Her silent, furious protests at feared chaos.

Two nights on. The man hears a movement, in the darkness. He walks into his eldest daughter's room. She is sitting bolt upright, still asleep, but with her eyes open. She says just this:

'Daddy.'

Then lies down again and is silent.

The next day, the younger child, who has been told nothing yet—who cannot possibly understand anything yet—says:

'Where's Daddy's house?'

Then she says:

'Daddy's crying, Mummy's crying, Ruby's crying, Cissy's crying.'

No one has cried in front of her. She is two and a half years old.

The man is not superstitious, but he shares Shakespeare's belief that misfortunes come not as single spies. Everywhere he looks, connections are being unmade—friends parting, death intruding, couples disintegrating.

Tim Lott

On one side of the house the neighbours are getting divorced, on the other side they have separated just this week. Another two friends have left or been left by their partners. The world seems to operate in these ebbs and surges.

On the fifth day, death begins to worry his elder daughter.

'You're not going to die, are you Daddy? I hope Mummy isn't going to die.'

She starts crying.

'What's it like to die, Daddy?'

'It's like going to sleep.'

This doesn't satisfy her.

'But…but then you don't wake up!'

And she cries bitterly once more. The man is lost for consolation, because what she says is so terrible and true.

Another time, she says:

'I want my real mummy.'

This daughter sometimes separates her parents into two. When her mother was angry with her, she would say: 'I want my good mummy,' thinking her bad mummy had appeared instead. Now she wants her real mummy, that is to say, the happy one.

Will I lose them? he wonders, for the hundredth time. Then he doesn't allow himself this thought any more. It scares him too much. He has never loved anything in his stupid life so much as his children. This, he supposes, is a banal, commonly repeated sentiment, but it is true, as true as anything can be.

The next night, the man thinks of other women he might hold in bed. But the thought doesn't excite him or interest him. He has always found his wife attractive, and the sex has been more than good. But he is numbed anyway by the prospect of that much intimacy.

He is frightened, but not nearly as frightened as he had thought he might be.

On the seventh day he studies bank balances. There is two months' money left. But he refuses to let it worry him. He has come to believe in putting a certain amount of faith in the future. Not an intemperate amount. Just so much. It's going to be tough though. Money, atypically he understands, is one of the things he and his wife never quarrelled about. Their arguments were more about deafness, their inability to hear each other, and blindness, their inability to see each other.

The eighth day. Illusion is always pecking at the edges of their separation. More than once, the woman says to the man:

'Well, we can still go out together.'

And he thinks but does not at first say:

No, no we can't.

Things have changed, more than them simply occupying a different physical space. They are separate now. They are in this weird non-place, where they are not lovers, but more connected than friends, but at the same time not friends. They are suddenly The Separated, a class of relationship which is uneasy and vexed.

The same day, the man buys the woman flowers, worrying about what will seem respectful and concerned without being romantic, that will show a common cause. Roses, carnations, tulips, lilies are all wrong. He settles in the end for ginger-flowers which are red, spiky, outside the normal run of things.

At times, she quizzes him.

Who have you told? What did they say? What did they think? Who did you tell today? Who did you tell yesterday?

He grows irritated. He is tired.

When he does tell his friends, there is no great surprise or shock as there was last time they parted. They have been nudged off the front page to the bottom of page five. It's a filler, a par. They are not fresh news. Probably people buried them a year ago, when they were unable to bury themselves. Nobody even seems sad. Nobody says, as they did before:

'Are you sure?' Or:

'What about the children?'

People now shrug as if it's no big deal. His male friends do seem not much bothered. They don't come around, don't call much. Embarrassed, perhaps. Bored, more likely. He is writing a book about male friendships. He thinks the writer's thought, the consolation, that always comes with pain:

Well. It's good material.

New ways of censoring emotions come to him. If he feels cheerful, he is afraid to show it, in case it is an affront to the woman, in case she thinks he is not grieving sufficiently. But the grief comes in fits and starts, in moments and shadows. The rest of the time, things are normal. They both can still laugh.

More than a week has passed now. He will soon move out of the house. The children need to be told. Both the man and his wife are frightened of this prospect.

The eldest girl is getting upset. She doesn't want to be in her own bed but to sleep with one of them. Tee repeats to himself over and over again the most fundamental lesson he has learned in his life—that nothing is good or bad of itself. That even the worst things can have good consequences sooner or later, and vice versa. That one cannot guess the result of one's actions, or describe what might have happened if those actions had not been taken. All one can ever do is respond to the demands of the moment and take the consequences as and where they fall.

The elder daughter says:

'I don't want to be married when I grow up, and I don't want to have children.'

He says:

'You don't have to if you don't want to. You don't have to marry anyone and you don't have to stay married if you do.'

That night, he can hear the couple next door shouting, screaming, throwing things at each other, and he remembers himself saying:

'You fucking cunt.'

The great communicator. He thinks: Do any of us have any hope of communicating finally? How do you do it? And how do you love? And are they, finally, the same thing?

Sometimes a fear runs through him like a gale. When you have been mad, as once he was, this fear can never leave you.

The ninth night, the elder girl walks into the living room.

'Why are you sleeping down here?'

'Because Mummy snores.'

She laughs, and goes back to bed.

His health is suffering. He's shot his back. He spends every night sitting, bathetically, with a packet of frozen peas strapped to the skin behind him. He will scream in pain for no apparent reason, shocking passers-by. It is as if the emotional pain is being displaced to his middle to lower spine.

He has developed a cough. On one occasion he hawks up a gobbet of crimson blood, which he holds on his fingertip and examines, fascinated at the iridescent quality of its colour. He has a mysterious rash on his foot which will not clear.

He reads sad books. Holocaust literature, then Harold Brodkey's *This Wild Darkness*, the story of the writer's dying from AIDS.

Another night. The woman is asleep. He has to avoid looking at her face. He glances at it, then glances away. She's wrapped in a tartan blanket like the one his parents used to wrap him in for car journeys. Perhaps it is even the same blanket—he cannot remember whether his mother gave it to him.

She hugs herself, dreaming. He looks away, for fear he will be overwhelmed by sadness. Her face is beautiful, he finds it beautiful, and sad. He wonders who she was. Now he supposes he shall never know, then thinks, too intellectually, defensively:

But what does the question mean?

He thinks: We blundered about together, trying to make some sense of things, to find an accord. Things were often a mess, but not always. There were fine times, clichés. Drunken Mediterranean summers. A day at the park with the kids. Just watching TV.

He thinks of John Updike's words—'growth *is* loss. There's no other way.'

His life has felt slightly unreal for a long while and he wishes it to take on the quality of reality. Already that is happening. Things are thickening, clarifying. Something is dying in him, something is embryonic. Perhaps that is the nature of every moment.

The evening of the next night, two days before the man is finally leaving the family home, the man and the woman have to tell the children what is happening. They have to think of a plausible story, that is true enough, but not incomprehensibly true.

The children are watching a cartoon, a videotape of *The Simpsons*, when the man comes in from his office. The man and woman snap at each other two, three times in the first few minutes. Both are nervous. They want to get it over with.

They leave the children watching the cartoon, then go downstairs and try to agree a party line—how much truth to tell, how much to withhold, how kindly they can tell certain truths, how some unkind truths must be shown. They cannot agree anything consistent, and mither and squabble. It is because of their fear.

The two parents sit down and pause the video. The man sets about it immediately. He tries to explain that they will now have two places to live instead of one. He dresses this up as an addition rather than a subtraction. He explains that their father will no longer spend the nights there, but at the other place. This place, he will show them tomorrow.

He takes them upstairs. It is actually possible to see the flats into which he is moving from the top-floor rear window. He points the building out to them, and the church spire that sits behind it. He says that they will be able to wave to him.

The elder child seems puzzled, but more or less unconcerned. The younger doesn't understand a word of what is being said. The most uncomfortable moment is when the elder looks up at the man, brightly, and says:

'Will you ever come and sleep here again?'

And he takes a deep breath and says firmly:

'No. Never.'

Such a crushing, bitter word. The girl says:

'Ohhhhh.'

In a small, disappointed way, as if denied a sweet or a piggyback.

The awful finality of it. But the girl doesn't seem to mind. The man feels worried that he has failed. He tries to explain to the girls, drawing on reserves of popular wisdom, that they're not 'to blame'. He simultaneously worries that even mentioning the word 'blame' might sow an idea that otherwise would have been absent. Also it suggests that something bad has happened, and this is not how they are presenting these events.

Everything's so delicate, like the inside of a ticking, sprung watch. The man is desperate to avoid letting loose the wrong words, which will somehow permanently imprint themselves in the children's minds. Demons may be created, may be conjured here, at this moment, in this room. So care, care.

After a while there seems to be nothing to say. The two girls grow restless. They turn back to the cartoon. His wife says, kindly:

'You did very well.'

And he feels so grateful for her support, and proud that he has managed. At the same time he knows that it is an infinitesimal first step, knows there are aching dark fields in front of the children that they do not realize or sense.

He tells the elder girl three times before she goes to bed that he will take her tomorrow to see the flat. She is excited.

The next day, the last but one, he takes the children up to the new place. It is on the top floor of a stucco terrace, with big picture windows overlooking West London. The sky is huge through these windows, dwarfing all else. The children are happy and excited. It is a nice flat, small. He brings toys to establish one room as their territory, spreads them out on the floor as if laying garlands. He worries as they run around that they will collide with the landlady's furniture.

The next day is an ordinary Saturday. The man takes the children to an adventure playground in the morning. In the afternoon, the woman takes them to a park. It is the man and the woman's last night together.

After the children have gone to bed, they open a bottle of champagne. Ess makes dinner, the last supper. It is a good evening, peculiarly relaxed. They try to celebrate the time they have had together, even now that it is finished. But after a while, the talk simply begins to run out. Silences now are already more insupportable than they were before, contain more tension and ungrounded electricity. The man thinks: You run out of road so quickly when there are no quarrels to bind you.

The woman says:

'Why don't we go upstairs and have a game of cards?'

Reassured by the banality of the idea, they go upstairs, but they can't find the cards. Nine o'clock. The woman decides to go to bed. The man gets ready to unfold the sofa bed. The last night under this roof. There's a moment when they almost have sex, but each knows it would be merely nostalgia. Yet both weaken nonetheless, but at different times, so it doesn't happen.

On the sofa bed that night, the man is surprised to find that he cannot locate a sense of tragedy inside him. He expects it, but it does not come. There is a deeper sense of the rightness of the course of events. Their marriage wasn't even a particularly bad one, he supposes. Neither was unfaithful to the other, they never fought about money, they never came to blows, they were both concerned with each other's welfare.

But for him communication is an obsession, a neurosis almost; without it he feels himself panting for breath, dying. The woman is cautious of it, finds it painful to give up too much of what her secret self believes and intuits. She has been hurt as a child, awfully.

He thinks: We each had different solutions to the solitude of our lives, and they did not mix. I battered on her door, threatening, or so it seemed to her. So she put on another bolt, and another.

The next morning the man is packing, putting everything into bags. It takes no time at all. The couple have an argument in the morning, one of the endlessly recurring ones, as recorded on paper, one of the arguments that landlocked them in the marriage. And he thinks to himself: Soon, we won't have to do this any more.

And relief again spreads throughout his body, like a small narcotic rush.

The end of the day. The girls have been put to bed. Just as the man makes to leave, with his baggage, he hears the elder one calling him back. He had thought her to be asleep.

He goes to her bedroom, and the girl, who is sitting up on a wooden bunk bed, grabs his single hand tightly with both of hers. And she looks at him, and at that moment on her child's face there is a look that seems to him like that of a grave adult. Her tiny fists. She looks him right in the eyes, and says: 'I love you, Daddy.'

This is something, unlike her young sister, she almost never says. I love you. It feels to the man as if someone or something is talking through her. Trying to reassure him, after all the reassuring he has been trying to do.

The girl lets go of his hand, lies down and closes her eyes.

February

It is Sunday in the man's new flat, where he lives now alone, without the clamour of a family, the tussles and screams and regular morning-to-dusk love and fury.

He thinks: Why did we get married?

People, he knew, thought that he and Ess were unsuited. Perhaps the two of them sought out each other's damage. Perhaps it was all just a genuine misunderstanding, an accident. But the explanation he prefers is this: that they didn't make a mistake, that they set out on a course together that had the seeds of its unhappy conclusion in it, but that was not the same thing. A failed marriage was not necessarily a mistake.

They had many good times, happy times. Helped as well as harmed each other. They had...an experience. They lived life, their own, each other's. They attacked each other, defended themselves, sometimes defended each other and attacked themselves.

What others called failure he thought of as life's essential roughage.

It changed him, the man thinks. It changed her, he hopes. The change was painful sometimes, certainly. But can that be cause for regret?

They have two daughters. This love burns as bright as phosphorus inside them both. Their adults' love, they hope, is not so far regressed that they would let their differences damage the children. But then they imagine that all newly separated couples have this belief, and many are found wanting all the same.

What was left between them, other than this insoluble glue? Concern for each other still, flickering affection. Anger of course, rivers, straits and oceans of it, that ever-present binder and repellent, directed at his 'laziness', her 'martyrdom', his 'selfishness', her 'compulsions'. The deeper cause was what the deeper cause always is, the man guessed—the mutual unwillingness to let go of the patterns of thinking and behaving that they mistakenly thought protected them from what it was they feared, what everyone fears: that they were not good people, that their very selves were in jeopardy, that nothing was certain. That they were not in control. □

DESTINY

Tim Parks

Destiny: there are those who still believe this word has meaning. One such is an old man who at seventy-plus decided he wasn't through with fighting his wife. What I want to know is what was going on in his head the moment he came down the stairs and with tears in his eyes announced to his son-in-law: 'This is my destiny.'

It is impossible to cram a life into the longest book, never mind a few pages. All the same, the dramatic scene in question may be prefaced by another. The son-in-law—let's call him Frank—is on the phone to his wife's brother, Angelo, son of the old man, whom we can refer to from now on as Babbo, Italian for Dad. The two young men, Frank and Angelo, one American, one Italian, are talking about the fact that the old folks want to divorce. Or say they do. Angelo's mother, Mamma, has demanded all the property, half Babbo's pension, plus whatever it costs to maintain their schizophrenic son, the eldest, now languishing in some closed community. On the phone, Angelo says he washes his hands of his parents. He refuses to see them. Or even talk to them. Babbo has always been a disgrace, he says, going after other women and letting Mamma know. He deserves everything that's coming to him. Frank points out that Mamma is a notoriously difficult woman to get on with: charming and irascible, ever quick to accuse and castigate, usually with slammed doors and sullen silences. 'She does have that hotel receipt,' Angelo remarks, referring to the affair Babbo is recently supposed to have had with an upstairs tenant, an unprepossessing creature of fortyish. 'Look,' Frank says, exchanging glances with his wife, Marta, the only daughter, who is standing at the open kitchen door, 'nobody is denying that Babbo has behaved badly, that he's screwed around, but he put you all through school and did everything for Stefano'—meaning the schizophrenic—'I can't see why you can't give him, or better still your mother, a bed for a night or two, because we can't handle having both of them here. Not at the same time.' Then when the phone is put down, to the immense surprise of both Frank and Marta, Babbo walks downstairs from where he has been listening on the landing. The younger couple had thought he was out picking up their little children from school. 'Thank you for defending me,' Babbo smiles, 'but please note that whatever stories may be told about me, I have never "screwed around", as you put it.' He seems immensely pleased with this dignified performance, so different from the shaken, tearful figure who will descend the same stairs the following afternoon.

In any event, you are beginning to get the picture. A life suppurating with unpleasant incident. A family where bygones are never bygones. Grudges, hatchets, corpses, are only buried the better to be dug up again. Decay seething with vitality. Babbo says he'll pop out to a hotel before Mamma arrives, as he did last time. Then for a few minutes he speaks ill of her, as she no doubt will of him when she arrives.

The last time—only a few days ago—was when Mamma came up north to visit the schizophrenic Stefano whose community is nearby. It was one of the rare occasions when he had permission to go out, though only if accompanied by both his parents. Since Babbo refused to go with her, she pretended her husband was waiting outside in the car because illegally parked. The community official was not taken in. Both parents must sign in person. Now Mamma is frantic that she will never be able to spend time with her son if Babbo refuses to cooperate. Just as it took two to procreate the boy— for she still thinks of this obese forty-five-year-old as a boy—it now takes two to have his company. Divorce becomes unfeasible. There is a knot somewhere that won't come undone. One way of dealing with such Gordian tangles, of course, is to wield a sharpened sword.

Thus Alexander the Great claimed vast new territories to his crown, thus countless others have abandoned their chains to explore new marriages, new predicaments: the blade hacks, the coils give, people are free to breathe and regret. Having been locked out of his house some six weeks ago, upon Mamma's discovery of the credit-card bill indicating payment for a double room in a nearby seaside hotel, Babbo claims to have reached this critical point. Since then he has been staying with his daughter Marta and son-in-law Frank. But while the great blade whirls and glitters round his balding head, somehow it never descends to sever the knot. The separation is not finalized. Indeed, Marta and Frank have begun to suspect that Babbo is merely trying to make Mamma jealous by monopolizing the grandchildren, particularly the delightful two-year-old daughter. Unless the truth is simply that nothing is less likely to lead to change, than talk of change. A destiny is cemented, perhaps, by dreams of happenstance and peripeteia. So at Gethsemane Christ prayed that he might be spared the crucifixion, well aware that this was not His Father's will.

Alternatively, there are those who claim such embroilments can, with patience, be disentangled. Even if only for examination. The experts, the therapists. The very American Frank, for example, disturbed to find the landscape he has married into thus pitted with shallow and decidedly unquiet graves, is attempting to get his bearings by reading a book called *Psychotic Games in the Family*— another metaphor for protracted conflict where exhumations and knotty hitches can now be seen, through an analyst's eye, as move and countermove in a deadlocked game. This notion puts Frank in mind that he may be able to blow the whistle on it all. 'Don't scuttle off to a hotel when Mamma comes again,' he tells his Italian father-in-law. 'That would be as much a sign of weakness as going away with her just because she came to get you. Then there'll never be an end to the story. Wouldn't it be better if I met her at the door and told her you don't want to see her, that you're serious about the divorce, and that she can stay with Angelo until it's sorted out?' Thus, some hours later, we have the telephone conversation already described, followed by Babbo's majestic, paunch-led descent down suburban stairs with declarations at once of innocence and resolution.

The central thesis of *Psychotic Games in the Family* is that the families of schizophrenic children are characterized by a long-running, never-to-be resolved antagonism between the parents, each of whom seeks to draw the unfortunate child into a privileged relationship with themselves against their partner. In his or her desire to grow up, the child welcomes this intimacy, only to sense at some later stage that he, or she, has been nothing more than a bargaining chip in the game being played out between father and mother. At which point, with a thousand other factors playing their part, disillusion and resentment may seek their inarticulate outlet in pathology.

Reading this heady material, Frank sees many parallels with what he knows about Marta's family and perhaps drawn by the idea of the game, as the mind is ever beguiled into creativity by analogy, he thinks of chess. Babbo and Mamma, whom he loves very much, are now long past the complex middle-game gambits that perhaps contributed to Stefano's schizophrenia. It's too late to undo that now, too late to say, 'If I just took back this or that move,' or, 'If only I had played a different opening.' No, these old folks are in one of those impossible endgame situations where neither white nor black can ever win, the kings roaming pointlessly across the squares, chasing and repelling each other, but without the power to make a kill. Time, then, to inform them that once the pawns are gone, the rules stipulate no more than fifty moves to stalemate. After which forces must be disengaged, the board closed.

Frank has high hopes.

That Mamma is indeed coming a second time the younger couple know because the old folk's neighbours, 300 miles away, have phoned to say that, after returning exhausted from her last attempt to visit her sick son, the old lady spent but a couple of days expressing her fury to all and sundry, then set off again. Early this morning. And where to, if not to Stefano and Babbo? Stefano via Babbo, Mamma would say. Though perhaps the truth is more Babbo via Stefano. In any event this initiative on the neighbours' part surprises no one. Every drama attracts—requires—its audience and stage crew. Without the spotlights, without the *schadenfreude* they vouchsafe to others, where would the actors find the energy to go at it with such demonic zeal? Would Hamlet's player have wept, without witnesses, for Hecuba? As Mamma strikes up the garden path, probably well aware she is expected, even observed, she looks exhausted, yes, and dishevelled, but at least she seems to know what she's about; she has rehearsed her part, and this gives her an air, if not of happiness, at least of determination, the grim satisfaction, even in disaster, of knowing who one is, and that others are paying attention. Christ, one feels, might have suffered less had His Father let the cup pass, but who would he have been without his crucifixion? Or Scott had he come back? Or Nelson without his 'kismet'—his fateful death at Trafalgar? And if none can be resurrected in the public mind unless they embrace their destiny, it goes without saying that an attentive audience can create a sense of purpose. Even if it apparently leads to calamity. Mamma will not disappoint.

But Frank is ready. Even before Mamma rings, he opens the front door and greets her as she climbs the condo stairs to their duplex. Gently, he asks her what she is doing, arriving unannounced. Usually she phones. And he suggests, as kindly as he can, that it would be better if she went to stay with Angelo, or in a hotel. Until things have been sorted out with her husband. For Babbo is serious, Frank tells Mamma, about separating. She brushes past him. Without removing her coat, she goes straight to the kitchen, opens the fridge, finds cheese, bread, wine. Perhaps aware she is in need of strength, she eats ravenously, scornfully. 'He's skulking upstairs, I presume?' And Mamma makes it clear she's not leaving without him. Without him she can't see Stefano, her first-born.

Mamma drinks off two tumblers of wine before Frank can remove the bottle. Marta is out, unfortunately, but he phones Angelo and asks him to come and help. Angelo prevaricates. Nevertheless, Frank feels quite sure of what he is about: these two people, he says to himself, Babbo and Mamma, do nothing but upset each other and those around them. It's time to help them to help themselves. He is experiencing that dangerous and peculiarly modern delirium of he who imagines that a little knowledge and related technique can dissolve decades of antagonism. Perhaps not unlike an American Secretary of State on a peace mission to Palestine.

At this point Frank's two young children come home from school. 'To think,' Mamma is shouting, 'how that bastard would kiss his own kids with his mouth still mucky from the knickers of his rotten sluts.' Frank objects that this is over the top and dispatches the children upstairs to watch television. She must go if she cannot desist from saying such things. She must go anyway, since Babbo does not want to see her. As he says this Frank is aware that Babbo, no doubt listening from the top of the stairs, will now have to contend with Japanese cartoons in the background: Ken Shiro, the technique of Okutu. 'You'll feel so much better once you've broken off this obsession,' Frank explains to his seventy-year-old mother-in-law. And adds that he's sure that after a little while of healthy separation Babbo will be more than ready to go with her to visit Stefano. Then, since no one in this family has ever really washed their hands of anything, Angelo arrives after all.

Could it be that everything that partakes of life, everything vital, is essentially unbalanced? Is this the scandal that underlies all others? That only the sick are interesting? That only suffering offers potential meaning, while nothing fills the existential void like the fizz of a neurotic mind, the back and forth of an embattled relationship? In any event Angelo tries to make light. 'Relax, Mamma. Come over to my place. We can go out to dinner together.' Mamma begins to rave. She will not leave without Babbo. What a miserable coward he is not to come downstairs to talk to her! Frank fixes her a glass of water with some drops of tranquilliser which she pretends to drink, but in fact pours out into the children's goldfish bowl. 'Those whom God hath joined together,' she shrieks, 'let no man put asunder!'

Then Frank raises the stakes. He says that if Mamma will not go willingly, he will throw her out, or even call the police. If nothing else, the book he has been reading has given him a sense of the strength of the forces at play in such situations. But perhaps distracted by the text's therapeutic vocation, he has overlooked one of the deeper messages: that the parents of schizophrenics, while rarely serene, are not necessarily unhappy in their eternal antagonism. Or at least not unspeakably so. Rather, and quite movingly, these embattled couples seem to need each other, not unlike the quarrelling figures in Beckett's plays who ever announce they have had enough, but never leave. That a third human being may be destroyed by this mechanism is a terrible thing, but it doesn't undo the fact that such partners draw their lifeblood from each other's veins. Mutually succouring vampires, their teeth are snugly set at each other's necks. 'I'll kill myself rather than leave without him,' Mamma screams, and seizes the bread knife.

But what is Babbo thinking upstairs? For it's his mental processes I am interested in, not Mamma's determined melodrama. She knows what she wants, he hesitates. Or appears to. Presumably he is aware of a variety of possible decisions. Is he gratified, as he listens, by her determination to have him? Does it offer a sense to his life? Or is he appalled? Or both? Is he just waiting to see if she will go before he caves in? Or is he thinking of the woman he had the affair with? If he did. Or of other women as well? Perhaps his life is a garden infested with might-have-beens, the way some amateurs can never decide which of three plants must go so that one can grow properly. Could it be, then, that Frank is wrong? That it is not so much a question of the old man's never having been able to leave his wife, as of his never being able serenely, finally, to choose her. Or to feel—for this is another alternative—that he has no choice.

Babbo scratches at a freckled baldness, turns to the TV screen where an expert in obscure martial arts is saving at least the world, perhaps the universe. The children gape. If living means being in thrall to the enchantment of the possible—'where there's life there's hope'— then a sense of destiny will presumably involve surrender to the only possible, an acceptance of mortality: this is my one life, my one adventure, the one woman between myself and death. But should we be obliged to *choose* our destiny, rather than merely grasping a sense of it after all is settled? Or rather, if we choose it, was it really destiny? Or just a mistake? Boswell quotes Samuel Johnson as remarking that the overall sum of human weal and woe would not be greatly altered if marriages were imposed by the public registrar. And our immediate thought on reading those words is that Johnson is trying to tell us that random selection is as good, and bad, as pondered choice when it comes to the pairing of men and women, that one cannot know with whom one will be happy, or indeed with whom one might have had a profitable unhappiness. But looked at another way, perhaps what Johnson meant was that if only our partner had been imposed, had been perceived as fate rather than choice, we would not fret so. The way few fret because they were born male, or female, or found themselves growing up in Asia, or in Edinburgh. One's partner would be accepted as part of the landscape, something to come to terms with: in fine weather congenial; dismal in the thin rain of November; under storm clouds menacing. Downstairs there is a loud shriek and the sound of a scuffle.

Then how is it—and Babbo once shared this thought with Frank, with whom he has often sought complicity against Mamma in the couple's age-old game of seducing third parties in order to hurt and keep each other—how is it that having chosen something, it may come, over the years, to seem imposed upon us, like the most terrible edict from the highest authority? So that one has both the responsibility of the choice and the impotence of the victim. This is discouraging, but might at least have led to resignation, had not the can of worms been opened again by the possibility of divorce. All recent development—social development—in the West has been worthily directed towards 'increasing individual choice', giving us 'control over our lives', reducing the incidence of imposed destiny. And yet…'Do not offer a three-year-old a choice of diet,' says the child-psychology book I have been reading, 'the burden of deciding is too much for him.' But at what age is it not too much? Contraception, abortion, euthanasia—the Pope knows we are not ready for them, as we were never really ready, perhaps, to have the sacred texts in our native tongue. If we have to decide things for ourselves, or illude ourselves that that's the way things work, then who shall we blame when things go wrong? True, psychoanalysis has offered us the alibi of parent-induced complexes: I continue to make awful choices in life because I was brought up by these monsters (young Angelo makes ample use of this expedient when his various relationships fail). But it is a poor and tortuous determinism to substitute for, say, the edict of an oracle: the boy will kill his father, marry his mother; or for a caste system that allows you to claim: I am here, like it or not, because I was born to this; I am beside this woman, like it or not, because, under the direction of our household gods, our families chose each for the other. The more shape is imposed, the freer I am in my mind to reflect upon it. That said, one would not wish to be walled in a cell.

Downstairs Mamma is screaming. She has turned the knife not on herself, but on Frank, who had picked up the phone, though more as a bluff than because he has really decided to call the police. Angelo, reassured to find his own considerable personal problems once more explained by the madness of his parents, is trying to wrest the weapon from her. Meanwhile, upstairs, while the children watch their cartoon, Babbo still paces back and forth, mulling over and over an ancient stalemate. He was brought up in the Twenties and Thirties. There was no divorce in Italy then, nor any real prospect of economic ease. Wartime soldiering imposed on him that relief in submission to destiny which no doubt explains why men and women will risk their lives for causes whose outcomes can hardly be of great personal interest to them. Perhaps his happiest period was in an American

POW camp, studying English, building military airports. After which, the general rush to marry old girlfriends.

Now, quite suddenly, the child-rearing over, even the necessity to earn over, he finds himself in a world where everything can be renegotiated, where people are learning to live in a constant delirium of choice and possibility. And Frank, his son-in-law, whom he respects, has insisted that it is merely a matter of holding firm. He can have what he wants, what he sometimes imagines he wants, his slippered independence in a quiet little flat somewhere. Away from her. It's just that now the crisis is upon him, the final decision, he finds himself paralysed. Not quite convinced by either the old world or the new, he has the worst of both: the sense, that is, that it would be possible to rearrange his life, if only he were someone else. For the destiny of being oneself, ultimate and unavoidable imposition, is never more humiliatingly evident than when all other constraints are stripped away. A cry and the sound of a body falling start his feet walking down the stairs.

First his shoes appear, then his baggy trousers, tightening towards the paunch. Does he hope that something awful has happened that will decide matters for him? A catastrophe? Now his sweat-stained shirt is in view, now his heaving chest. Does his descent represent a collapse of resolution, a defeat, the inability to imagine another self? Or a triumph of responsible decision: I choose this life, this woman, whatever the drawbacks may be? Did he ever really mean anything more in all this melodrama than to make her see she needed him? By hurting her? To push things to the limit? Whatever the truth, his face, when it comes into view, appears to be melting: his eyes are melting, even the skin seems to be melting from his jowls and neck. Frank, who has just helped the now disarmed Mamma to her feet, is appalled. He genuinely wanted to help his father-in-law, but the experience seems to have reduced Babbo to some kind of ghoulish jelly. 'You can't give in now,' Frank protests. His Italian is accented with American. 'It's blackmail. She throws a tantrum and you do what she says.' Babbo cannot look the younger man in the eyes. He is moving slowly and deliberately, as though in a trance. 'This is my destiny,' he announces. And repeats, 'My destiny.'

The parents of my own sister-in-law, in the United States,

Tim Parks

married, divorced, remarried, then divorced again. One reads more and more often of this kind of thing. The mind is liquid, fickle. Who is not familiar with its fast swinging tides, its sudden kaleidoscopic rearrangements of the past? Speaking of beliefs, causes, commitments, the ferocious Max Stirner, forerunner of Nietzsche, was quick to scorn people for wanting nothing better than something they could enslave themselves to—religion, love, patriotism—for not having the courage, that is, to check at every turn of the road that their lives were exactly what they wanted. And indeed it may well be that secretly we seek nothing more of marriage—or work, or the city where we live—than to be securely locked away there. As many, entering some extravagant new supermarket, will close their minds and trust to old brand loyalties. On the other hand, who can deny that there must have been a certain serenity in a society that worshipped its ancestors and imposed what it imagined was best on its children? Alone in his living room—Babbo, Mamma and Angelo having gone now, even laughing together surprisingly on the stairs— the disillusioned Frank is left behind in his contemporary world where one must choose one's happiness every day: choose where one lives, choose one's wife, choose whether the children go to state school or private; a world where no social scaffolding can disguise the fact that one's destiny is none other than this uncertain stranger, oneself: 'chameleon despite himself', as Beckett describes his hero Molloy. Could it be that Frank will some day envy Babbo and Mamma? In the kitchen one of two goldfish floats slowly to the surface. Another victim. □

THE MISTRESS
Dani Shapiro

Here, in no particular order, are some things Lenny told me: that he and his wife didn't sleep in the same bed; that they hadn't had a 'real marriage' in years; that she was undergoing electro-shock treatment in a clinic outside Philadelphia; that he had cancer, and had to fly to Houston three days a week for chemotherapy; that his youngest daughter, aged three, had a rare form of childhood leukaemia. That he could not get a divorce for all of the above reasons. That he was heartbroken that he could not leave his wife and marry me.

For a long time, I believed him. With every bone in my body, I trusted that Lenny Klein was telling me the truth. When we talked about it, his jaw would tighten and his big brown eyes would fill with tears. His voice would quaver with pent-up, complex feelings that I couldn't possibly begin to understand. Poor Lenny! I marvelled that so many bad things could happen to one person, and I vowed to take care of him. Writing late at night in my extensive journals, I exhorted myself to be a real woman—one who could step up to the plate and be good to her man in his moment of crisis.

Years later—now—I hold Lenny's lies up to the light and examine my own reasons for believing what, in retrospect, seems preposterous. I reread my old journals and notice the way my girlish handwriting deteriorated into a scrawl as I wrote: *I have to be there for Lenny. He needs me, and he is going through so much. I don't know if I can handle it—but I have to be strong!* I try to remember that Lenny was a trial lawyer, that he built an international reputation based on his own pathology: that he lied with an almost evangelical conviction. He prided himself on being able to convince anyone of anything.

Paris, 1985. We are walking along the Boulevard St Germain on a cloudless spring day. The rooftops of the Left Bank are creamy against a rare blue sky, and the air outside Café Flore smells of croissants and the acrid smoke of Gitanes, but I don't notice. Only now, as a grown woman, can I take in the rooftops of Paris, the extraordinary sky; I realize that in recalling this scene I am supplying it with a collage of my own more recent memories. In Paris, in 1985, I see only what is within one square foot of me, too busy feeling the complicated stew of sensations being with Lenny provokes. I am hung-over, floating on a wave of last night's Puligny-Montrachet and

DANI SHAPIRO BY JEFFREY NEWBURY

a four-star dinner that wound up in the toilet of the Hotel Ritz. Lenny's arm is around me, thick and proprietary, and it reminds me of the sex we had that morning, the way he pinned me to the bed and didn't let me move my arms until I came in spite of myself. In Paris, I am like an animal curled in a patch of sunlight, interested only in the beating of my own heart. Sex, wine, food, sleep. I am a physical being, living on the other side of a clear, thin membrane which separates me from anything to do with the world.

I have not read a newspaper or spoken to a soul other than Lenny for weeks now. I have been living the kind of unbelievable life people glide through in airport novels. We have been to London, Monte Carlo, the Côte d'Azur. I have played blackjack in private clubs with oil sheikhs who asked me to blow on their dice for good luck; I have driven a convertible around the hairpin turns of the Moyenne Corniche; I have eaten langoustine on a boat floating somewhere off the shores of Cap d'Antibes. I wear dark glasses and haute couture suits, a gold watch and a long, thick strand of pearls. I have no idea who I am.

Lenny steers us on to a narrow side street off the Boulevard St Germain, and into a children's clothing store filled with the embroidered dresses my mother used to buy me as a child. He tells me he wants to buy a dress for his youngest daughter, the one with the rare form of leukaemia. I help him look through racks of tiny dresses suitable for a three-year-old, until we find one he deems perfect, a pale yellow silk smock with a Peter Pan collar. He holds it up to the sunlight, and his eyes fill with tears. She'll never live to grow out of this dress, he whispers. My baby girl.

He has layered his lies one on top of the other until they have become opaque, an elaborate construction resembling reality. He is fond of quoting probably the only line he knows from Franz Kafka: *White is black and black is white*, he often says with a sigh. I never knew exactly what he meant by this, but it seemed to have a lot to do with my life at that time.

The lies had small beginnings. Lenny called me from a business trip and told me he was at Montreal airport, waiting to catch a flight to Calgary. I checked with the airline and found out that the flight would take approximately five hours. So when Lenny called an hour later to say he had landed in Calgary, I very calmly asked him where he really was.

'Calgary,' he said.

No, Lenny, really.

He stuck to his story. In the time that I knew him he never, ever changed his story midstream. I hung up on him and called his family's house in Westchester. When the maid answered the phone, I asked to speak with Mr Klein. And when he picked up the extension and I heard his rough, craggy *hello?* I screamed so hard into his ear that he dropped the receiver.

He raced into the city. He let himself into my apartment and found me curled up in bed. He scooped me up and held me to his chest. His wife wasn't home, he told me. She was having shock treatment. And someone had to take care of his daughter. He hadn't wanted to tell me because he'd wanted to spare me, to protect me from the horror of his life. Surely I understood. *Ssshh, sweetheart,* he murmured into the top of my head as I wept, my face beet red like a little girl's. *So many people need me,* he said, *but I love you best of all.*

On our first date, Lenny Klein took me to the River Café, an expensive restaurant in Brooklyn with sweeping views of the Manhattan skyline. It was only when we were halfway there, driving downtown in Lenny's Rolls Royce, that I realized I was on a date with my friend Jess's stepfather, and that we were not, as I thought, going to be planning a surprise party for her.

If only lives could be played out on movie screens, if only I could re-enter the precise moment when Lenny Klein picked me up for the first time, and edit it—I would take the girl I was, that girl speeding along the East River, and shove her out of the car.

At the River Café Lenny handed the maître d'hôtel a folded twenty dollar bill. I had never seen anyone do this before. My father had always made reservations at restaurants, and waited patiently at the bar if his table wasn't ready. Lenny and I were led to a window table with a candle flickering next to a small vase of pale pink roses.

'Did you see that?' Lenny asked me once we were seated.

'See what?'

'The way you turned every head in the place. Don't tell me you don't know the effect you have.'

The truth was that I hadn't noticed anyone looking at me, and I didn't quite believe Lenny.

'Do you know what I told Jess the first time I met you?' Lenny asked huskily, then continued, 'I told her you were a golden girl. A perfect angel.'

I flushed and looked down at my hands folded in my lap. I didn't know what to say. My last date had been with a senior named Adam, who brought along a six-pack of Coors and tried to feel me up outside my dorm door.

Lenny produced a pair of bifocals, then skimmed his finger down the wine list, frowning slightly.

A captain appeared at his side.

'Can I be of service with the wine list, sir?'

'Do you have a '58 Margaux?' Lenny asked. 'I see the '61, but—'

'I'm sorry sir, we have only the '61.'

'Very well, then.'

Lenny leaned back in his seat and smirked at me.

'This wine is older than you are,' he said.

I knew what I needed to do. I knew that I would be sunk if I didn't say something—and soon—about Jess, or about his wife. Not to speak up was to become Lenny's accomplice in whatever it was we were doing. But I felt paralysed, and beneath that paralysis there was a frisson of excitement, an awareness of doing absolutely the wrong thing.

Lenny sniffed the cork and watched the wine being decanted with all the fascination and reverence of watching a ballet. He swirled it around in his glass, took a sip, then gave a nod.

'Pour just a bit for the young lady,' he said. 'It needs to breathe.'

When the captain left, Lenny lifted his glass slightly in my direction.

'To beauty,' he said.

I flushed more deeply and looked out of the window at a boat moving slowly up the East River. I had an inkling of how much this excited Lenny: young girl, old wine. For the first time in my life I felt my youth as power. (In years to come, Lenny would turn to me and ask how old I was: twenty, twenty-one, twenty-two, I would answer with a perverse sort of pride, knowing that my age acted as an aphrodisiac, knowing that his beautiful wife was, at forty, too old for him.)

I drank the wine and felt it slide smoothly down my throat, warming the tightness in my chest. I had no experience of the ritual of drinking fine wine. In New Jersey, growing up, I thought of red wine as the sweet Manischewitz we sipped out of thimble-sized silver goblets on Shabbos.

After the Muscovy duck, after the crème brûlée and cognac, Lenny leaned across the table and ran his finger down my nose in a gesture at once paternal and sexual.

'I'll drive you home,' he said with a wink.

Inside his car, I sat all the way over against the passenger door as he drove me back to Sarah Lawrence, my cheek hot against the cool window. I felt sick to my stomach. I thought of Jess, back at school. How would I ever tell her I had gone out on a date with her stepfather? Would she ever forgive me?

Lenny fiddled with the dial of the radio until he found a jazz station. A throaty trombone filled the quiet between us. Then, on a long straight stretch of road, he reached down, slowly and deliberately moved my long skirt up my thigh, and squeezed my knee. I knew I should tell him that I couldn't ever see him again, but somehow it already seemed too late.

Two years have passed, and something has gone wrong, terribly wrong, with my life. I don't, in fact, think of my life as 'my life' but rather as a series of random events that have no logical connection. I am no longer a student. I dropped out of Sarah Lawrence after my junior year, supposedly to pursue acting. And I'm actually doing a pretty good imitation of an actress. You might even say that I'm playing the part.

But I'm doing an even better imitation of a mistress. Lenny has been busy buying me things. I don't particularly want these things—but they seem to be what Lenny is offering in lieu of himself. So, quite suddenly, overnight really, I find myself driving a black Mercedes convertible. And just in case I might be mistaken for anything other than a kept woman, I wear a mink coat, a Cartier watch, a Bulgari necklace with an ancient coin at its centre. The Mercedes is a step down from the first car Lenny gave me, when we had been going out for a month: a leased Ferrari. I didn't know how to drive a stick shift, so the Ferrari was a bit of a problem. What I must have looked like! A twenty-year-old blonde dressed like Ivana Trump, stalled in traffic, grinding gears, trying to find the point on the clutch to hold that ridiculous car in place.

Lenny rented an apartment on a pretty little street in Greenwich Village, a furnished triplex with a garden, a fireplace, and a bedroom with a four-poster bed. He called it 'our house', as if he didn't have another home with a whole family in it an hour north of the city; he kept half a dozen suits in the bedroom closet, and a brand-new silk robe hung behind the bathroom door. There was an entire floor we didn't use—a large, airy children's nursery.

My parents knew that something was up. They knew I was going out with somebody, but they had no idea who. I was drifting away from them—and they were letting me go. One night I invited them over for dinner. I pushed all traces of Lenny out of sight. But of course there were clues: a glossy brochure for Italian yachts; a humidor in the centre of the coffee table; a man's Burberry overcoat on a hook near the front door.

I cooked up a storm, and the place was filled with homey smells: garlic, basil, coriander. It was winter, and snow was piled up on the sills. Spotlights in the backyard shone on the landscaped garden, the redwood table, the Adirondack-style chairs and the huge terracotta pots of last spring's dead geraniums. I had my father's favourite music—Dvořák's Symphony for the New World—playing on the stereo system.

My parents rang the doorbell. They looked so solid standing on my front stoop, their cold, red noses poking out from above their mufflers. If nothing else, they looked like they belonged together. They were elegant and rangy, similarly proportioned. (Unlike Lenny and me. Lenny is thick as a linebacker, and I had become so delicate the wind could have picked me up and blown me away.) My mother strode into the brownstone as if it wasn't the weirdest thing in the world to be visiting her daughter in a lavish apartment with no name on the outside buzzer. My father trailed behind her warily, as if setting foot on another planet.

My mother entered the living room, flung her arms wide and did an impromptu dance to Dvořák.

'Tra-la-la, tra-la-la,' she trilled.

My father and I hung back and watched, our faces crumpled into awkward smiles. We were used to it. In every family there is room for only one Sarah Bernhardt, and my mother had assumed that role. It didn't occur to me that she was frightened—that this was a lot for her to take in, her college drop-out daughter living in the lap of luxury. All I could see was her outsized self, twirling around my living room in her fur coat and boots.

I wanted a drink. I walked over to my mother and put a hand on her shoulder, and she spun to a halt. I took her coat, and my father's, and hung them above Lenny's raincoat by the front door. For the first time I noticed that there was a wreath made of twigs, a bit of Americana, on the wall near the kitchen, and I wondered if I could remove it quickly before my father saw it. Wreaths, under any circumstances, are as goyish as it gets. Which would be worse for my father? Imagining that I was with some powerful guy old enough to be my father? Or the possibility that the guy wasn't Jewish? I wished I could reassure him. Yes, Daddy. He's Jewish. Twenty-three years older than me, a pathological liar, married to a woman who knows nothing of me—and a Jew.

I poured two glasses of Chardonnay for my parents and a large vodka for myself. I figured that if the vodka was in a water glass they wouldn't know the difference—especially if I drank it like it *was* water. My drinking had taken on a new urgency in the past few months. It was no longer a question of desire but of need. I could not get through an evening like this without the armour of booze. I handed them their wine, and directed them to the couch. On the coffee table, I had put out a plate of crudités and a bowl of olives.

'Quite a place,' my mother said brightly, her gaze darting around the room at the white brick fireplace with its wrought-iron tools, the glass wall overlooking the garden, the soaring ceiling. My father stared at the fringe of the rug, glassy-eyed. He needed to be as numbed as I did to get through this night.

'Thanks,' I murmured, as if she was paying me a compliment.

I checked on dinner, using the opportunity to gulp some wine from the open bottle in the fridge. Vodka and white wine was a combination I knew worked for me. If I stuck with the formula, things shouldn't be too bad in the morning. It would only become a problem if I switched to red or had cognac after dinner. I had learned to colour-code my booze: clear (vodka, white wine) and coloured (scotch, cognac, red wine) weren't to be mixed. Especially if I wasn't eating. And I couldn't see myself eating.

I had prepared my signature dish. It was my signature because it was literally the only thing I knew how to cook. A recipe out of *The Silver Palate* cookbook, it was a chicken stew of sorts, with white wine, olives, prunes and brown sugar. I was serving it with wild rice and a string bean casserole I had bought ready-made at Balducci's. For dessert, a *tarte tatin* from Pâtisserie Lanciani. I had run all over the West Village preparing for this evening, thinking that my parents would be impressed by my culinary efforts, so impressed that, by the end of dinner, patting their full stomachs, they'd swell with pride at their only daughter who was, after all, living such a gracious and well-appointed life.

'Can I help?'

My mother was standing in the doorway. How long had she been there? Did she see me take the swig from the bottle of wine? I tried to think of explanations. Thirsty was the only word I could think of. But then I realized that she hadn't seen a thing.

'Actually, I think everything's under control,' I said, carrying the casserole to the table, which I had set with linen place-mats and napkins. In the centre of the table there was a vase of drooping purple tulips.

The silverware, the pots and pans, the linens were all courtesy of the owner of this sub-let place, a woman who I might—if I had been thinking of such things—have viewed as a cautionary tale. A blonde, whippet-thin, fiftyish real-estate broker, she had lines around her mouth that weren't from smiling. She occasionally stopped by

to fix something in the garden or the basement, and when I got near her I could smell vodka and stale nicotine just beneath a cloud of L'Air du Temps.

The music had stopped by the time we all sat at the dining room table, but I didn't notice then. If I had, I would certainly have changed the tape, filled the air with something other than the tinny, lonely sound of our three forks scraping against plates. I pushed my chicken from one side of my plate to the other; my stomach clenched and growled in protest. I had allowed myself one glass of wine in front of my parents, using a crystal wineglass from the set Lenny had bought me as a house-warming gift. It was all I could do not to down it in a single gulp.

It seemed that my parents and I, after twenty-two years in each other's company, had run out of things to say. I already knew their views on the political situation in Israel, and we couldn't discuss my school work—I was no longer in school. My father pressed a corner of his napkin to his lips and murmured something about the food being delicious. My mother agreed.

'My wonderful daughter,' she said, shaking her head. 'You've turned into such a little homemaker.'

I looked at my parents across the table. Is that what they really thought? How could they just sit there? Some small piece of me wanted my father to fling me over his shoulder and carry me, kicking and screaming, to the car he had parked outside. I secretly wished that they would drive me home to Hillside, deposit me in my childhood bedroom and feed me chicken soup and saltines. I wanted to start my life over again, but I didn't know how.

I was afraid that I was going to cry, so I walked into the kitchen and pulled the apple tart from its box, arranging it on a cake platter. What had I expected from this evening? I thought I wanted my parents to be proud of me, to see that I was living like an adult. But even I knew that this wasn't true. We were all playing a game here, pretending that this was a nice family moment: mother, father and daughter eating an elegant meal.

I presented dessert with a flourish. The *tarte tatin*, with fresh espresso from the brand-new espresso-maker. Finally, the conversation— if that is what you call the words we spread over the gaps—veered, like the tide, in the only direction it could.

'Can't you tell us,' my mother asked, as I took one bite of the delicious, flaky, apple tart, then another, and another. I was ravenous, like a starving dog. I'd make myself throw up later. 'Can't you tell us,' my mother asked, 'who he is?'

My father cleared his throat. 'It's been so long, Dani—it seems we really ought to know...'

I kept shovelling pieces of apple and crust into my mouth. I could actually feel my stomach closing around each morsel of food. The directness of their curiosity made me panic. My parents had been strangely passive on the subject of my dropping out of college and taking up with a mystery man. Over the past year I had returned from trips to Europe bearing gifts for them: Charvet silk ties for my father, brightly printed Pucci scarves for my mother. These were gifts I couldn't possibly have afforded to buy on my meagre income from the few television jobs I got. Who did they think paid for them? And why did they accept them? Part of me was screaming to tell them, to just get it over with. After all, they had met Lenny on Parents' Day, when he came to see Jess. They knew who he was. Had he, even for a moment, crossed their minds as a possibility?

His name was on the tip of my tongue. It would have been so easy. It's Lenny Klein, I could have said, then watched the chips fall. Would they have been horrified—or relieved? What could they possibly be imagining? I was woozy from the vodka, wine and the two helpings of apple tart. OK, I thought to myself. Just say it.

'Is it Teddy Kennedy?' my mother asked. She was joking. It must have been a joke. But I could see that she had really considered this. She looked at me. Did she want it to be him? An image of the bulbous-nosed, red-faced senator from Massachusetts flashed through my head. My mother was staring at me, wide-eyed, poised for an answer, and suddenly I couldn't seem to say anything at all.

Lenny was in the middle of litigating a famous case, and there was front-page coverage in the *New York Times* and the *Wall Street Journal*. In these pieces he was referred to as 'flamboyant' and 'feisty'. One reporter likened him to a bulldog, and another referred to his fleet of Ferraris and his trademark raccoon coat. Some people might not have welcomed this kind of coverage, but Lenny loved it. Just in case I missed any articles or photographs, Lenny had a messenger drop off clips each evening with my doorman. He'd never taken a case he couldn't win—and I guess he thought he could win me too, if only he was persistent enough.

After all, in the face of the most tangible proof that Lenny had been lying to me all these years, I remained with him. The simple facts about Lenny—who, what, when, where—had always been elusive to me, impossible to grasp as he slipped and slid his way around the truth like a snake in a river. *My little girl is dying*, he would say whenever I noticed the discrepancies in his stories, or: *My children's mother is having electro-shock therapy*. When I couldn't take my own confusion any more (Was Lenny lying to me? Was I going crazy?) I decided to hire a detective to get to the bottom of it. By this time my parents knew all about me and Lenny, in theory; but it wasn't something we could talk about.

When I think back to my younger self riffling through the New York City *Yellow Pages* in search of a private investigator, I feel like I'm watching a movie about someone else, a girl so clueless that she really didn't know that her desire to hire a detective was all the answer she needed. I chose a detective agency based on nothing more than its good address, in the East Sixties—a neighbourhood filled with private schools and shrinks. Most other agencies listed were in the Times Square area, or the Bronx.

It was a cool, crystal-clear spring day. I rang the ground-floor buzzer of a brownstone. A burly middle-aged man in a sports coat and polyester pants opened the door and ushered me inside. He had a thick head of sandy hair and fleshy pockets beneath his eyes. He looked exactly like my idea of a detective. I even noticed a trench coat hanging on a rack which stood by the door. He pointed me towards a small office furnished with a big library desk and two wooden chairs. The desk was covered with papers, and half-opened manila folders with the edges of photographs peeking out. An old-fashioned phone, the kind with the dial instead of push-buttons, sat on a pile of magazines.

'Mrs Shapiro?'

'Ms,' I replied faintly.

He blinked.

'I'm John Feeny,' he said. 'We spoke on the phone.'

For this scene I had dressed as conservatively as I knew how, as if, again, I were playing a role: pants suit, heels, and the pearls Lenny gave me for my twenty-first birthday. My hair was pulled back into a ponytail, around which I had wrapped a silk scarf.

'What can I do for you?' Feeny asked, not unkindly.

'You said on the phone that you sometimes deal with...personal business,' I said. 'I have a sort of weird situation.'

He leaned back and rested his head in his hands, smiling as if to assure me that no situation could possibly be too weird.

'Ms Shapiro,' he said. 'I was a detective on the New York City police force for twenty-five years before I opened my own shop. And I've been at this here thing'—he waved his hand around the room—'for a decade. Whatever it is, I'm sure I can deal with it.'

I suddenly became afraid. Lenny's face could sometimes bulge with rage, and I remembered a story he liked to tell about how he had once picked up a broken bottle from the street and slashed a would-be mugger's face. Lenny was sort of a public person. More public all the time. I wondered if I was about to get myself into a whole lot of trouble. But still, I didn't get up, thank Feeny for his time, and head for the door. I stumbled on.

'This isn't what you think,' I said. 'I'm in a relationship with a married man. And I want you to find out if my boyfriend is cheating on me with his wife.'

At this, Feeny's eyebrows shot up.

'Come again?'

'He claims his wife is in a mental hospital. He told me he hasn't been with her in years.'

'And you think he might be lying,' said Feeny. Did I see the laughter behind his eyes, or is my memory supplying it now, because I simply cannot imagine a middle-aged man listening to an earnest, overdressed twenty-two-year-old girl tell him that she thinks her boyfriend might still be sleeping with his wife?

'Yes,' I said.

'What's your boyfriend's name?'

'I'm a bit nervous telling you that.'

'Ms Shapiro, if you don't tell me his name I can't possibly help you. What, is he some kind of famous guy?'

'Well, sort of,' I said.

We stared at each other for a moment.

'His name is Leonard Klein, he's—'

'I know who he is,' Feeny responded drily. 'The lawyer guy.'

I nodded, then sat there, my hands folded in my lap.

'So what do you want? You want him followed?'

'I don't know,' I faltered.

'You want pictures? Video? Tape? You want his phone bugged?'

I actually began to get excited. After years of trying to figure Lenny out myself, here, finally, was someone who was going to do it for me.

'Everything,' I answered giddily. 'I want everything.'

'It's going to cost you.'

'How much?'

Feeny pulled a pocket calculator out from somewhere beneath the mess on his desk.

'Where does Klein live?'

'Upper Westchester.'

'So there'll be travel. You want us to stake out his house?'

'Yes.'

'OK.' He peered at the calculator. 'I'll need a retainer. And I'm going to have to put a few guys on this. So why don't we say five grand?'

I panicked. That was about the total I had saved of my own money. Everything else was what Lenny had given me: jewellery, a car, clothes, even cash from time to time. He had got me a credit card by lying to the bank, telling them I worked for his law firm. I had steadily been making less and less over the last couple of years; even my parents figured that Lenny was supporting me.

'Fine,' I said quickly.

I had no idea whether it was a fair price for what Feeny was going to do, or even how I'd survive once I paid him. But I needed to know the truth about Lenny as if my life depended on it.

'Where's Klein now?' Feeny asked as he took the cheque.

'In Europe,' I answered, 'on a business trip. He's due back

tomorrow on the Concorde from Paris.'

'Fine,' he said. 'We'll start there.'

Two days later, Feeny called to tell me that the passenger list for the Air France Concorde—no easy score, he assured me—showed a Mr and Mrs Leonard Klein travelling together. And the guy he sent to Kennedy Airport had spotted Lenny and his wife at the baggage claim. The photos were being developed.

Many things had occurred to me, but not this. I hadn't imagined for a moment that Lenny might be in Europe with his wife. Before he left on this trip he had given me a hotel number, and an associate in his law firm answered the phone at the Ritz each time I called. (I later found out that Lenny made a practice of this: he would fly a Harvard or Columbia Law School graduate across the Atlantic, check him into a hotel room, and instruct him what to say if I called.) Lenny had often told me his European business trips were top secret: meetings with Margaret Thatcher at 10 Downing Street, encounters with Russian spies.

In tears, I called my mother.

'I found out that Lenny was in Europe with his wife,' I said.

'Oh, darling, I'm so sorry. Is there anything I can do?'

'I don't think so.'

A pause.

'Do you want me to call his wife?'

My mother and Mrs Klein had met each other at a few school functions back when none of this could have struck anyone as a remote possibility.

'Yes,' I said. 'Call her.'

'I'll do it right now,' my mother said.

I sat by the phone and watched the minutes tick by. I pictured Lenny's wife answering the phone with a chirpy hello, and my mother's slow, steady explanation of why she was calling. I had set in motion a chain of events which was now unstoppable. More than twenty minutes passed before my mother called me back.

'Well, I did it,' she said.

'You talked to her?'

The world felt unreal, hallucinatory.

'Yes. She called me a liar. She told me that she has a happy marriage to a man who travels a lot. That he's on his way to California. And I said, "No, he's on his way to see my daughter."'

My mother sounded proud of herself, immersed in the drama of the moment.

'How did she seem?' I asked.

'What do you mean?'

'Lenny's wife—was she angry?'

'No,' my mother said slowly. 'She just didn't believe me, Dani.'

I spent the rest of that day in a state of awful excitement. Something was going to happen. And when Lenny showed up that evening at the apartment we were still sharing in the West Village, I was ready. He put his bags down and gave me a hug.

'How was Paris?' I asked.

'Exhausting,' he said. 'Non-stop meetings.'

'Really.'

He looked at me oddly, but we didn't have time to get into it. The phone rang. My mother had given Mrs Klein the number at the apartment and suggested she find out for herself what her husband was up to.

Lenny picked up the phone on the kitchen wall.

'Hello?'

I watched him, and for the first and only time in the years I knew him, he looked genuinely surprised. He didn't say a word. He just listened for a few minutes, then hung up the phone.

'That was my wife,' he said.

I was silent.

'How did she get this number?'

I shrugged.

'I have to go.'

'I'd imagine,' I said faintly. My anger was giving me the fuel that I needed to stay strong, at least for the moment.

When Lenny slammed out of the apartment, I was certain that I would never see him again. I knew the truth now. It was staring me in the face, in the concrete form of flight lists and photos. And he knew that I knew. And besides, the whistle was blown. What could he possibly tell his wife?

This was it, I told myself. Absolutely, positively the end.

Dani Shapiro

It wasn't the end. Lenny still called ten, twelve times a day. He left messages on my answering machine. *Hello?* His voice filled my bedroom. *Fox? Are you there?* Sometimes he didn't say a word. He would stay on the line for as long as five minutes, just breathing. I know he thought that he could get to me again. But I was trying harder than I ever had before to stay away from him. Sometimes he would call in the middle of the night and wake me out of a deep sleep; my hand would reach reflexively for the phone. But I always managed to stop myself before it was too late.

Eventually, he did get to me again. And for the next year that we were together—three days here, four days there—my life became unrecognizable to me. I idly wondered what it would take to get me to leave him. I wondered about this over bottles of chilled white wine, or heavy glasses half-filled with scotch.

I was still wondering about it when I went to stay for a while at a health spa in California. The phone rang in my room one day. There had been a car crash on a snowy highway. My mother had eighty broken bones. My father was in a coma. They were lying in a hospital 3,000 miles away, and suddenly—in ways I could not have imagined seconds earlier—nothing else mattered. As I packed my bags, I remembered my mother twirling—dancing to Dvořák—through the doors of Lenny's brownstone, and the glassy look in my father's eyes. I prayed that my father wouldn't die disappointed in me, and I knew then what I had to do. □

JAKARTA
Sebastião Salgado

In 1900 Jakarta was a small colonial capital—the Dutch called it Batavia—
with a population of 300,000. Today more than nine million people live in
the city. These photographs record what may be the last of its
great booms. President Suharto, one of the boom's chief beneficiaries,
has proclaimed that Indonesia can never again return to the spectacular
growth rates which ended last year in financial collapse.

GRANTA

WHAT YOUNG MEN DO

Richard Lloyd Parry

What Young Men Do

A friend of mine in Jakarta, a television reporter for one of the big international networks, came back from Borneo last year with a photograph of a severed head. To be accurate, what he had was the video of a photograph; the man who had taken the original, a local journalist, had not wanted to hand the print over, and making a copy was risky because the photo labs were under surveillance. So the cameraman had zoomed in on it, and held the camera steady. A newspaper could never reproduce such an image, and in my friend's film it remained on the screen for only a second or two.

It was lying on the ground, appeared to be male, and was rather decomposed. It was more absurd than atrocious, with a Mr Punch leer and wild holes for eyes. It looked carnivalesque, something from Hallowe'en, but almost immediately it was gone and the film cut away to burned-out houses, and to soldiers stopping the car and confiscating tapes. If you weren't paying attention, you might not have realized what you had just seen. If you did, you would probably have thought to yourself: So that's what a severed head looks like—well, it's not so bad.

A few months later, in May, I went to Indonesia myself to report on the elections. It was the last few days of the official campaign, and thousands of teenage boys had occupied the streets of Jakarta in long, aimless parades of chanting and flag waving. There were three official parties, and each had its own colour, its own symbol and its own number. Red bull number two (the democratic party) and green star number one (the Muslim party) were on good terms, but when either encountered yellow banyan tree number three, the ruling party, there was jeering and scuffles which usually ended with burned cars, thrown rocks, water-cannons and tear-gas charges by the police. The government referred to the elections as the 'Festival of Democracy', and the atmosphere in the street marches was closer to that of a football crowd than a political rally. There were party T-shirts and bandannas, party pop songs, and the sky above the flyovers was full of kites.

My friend Jonathan made ravishing films of the rallies. The dominant colours (red, yellow or green) gave them a medieval quality, like battle scenes from the films of Kurosawa. In Jakarta, the newspapers kept a count of 'campaign-related deaths' which, by the official reckoning, were almost always the result of traffic accidents rather than social unrest. But every few days stories filtered through of more sinister trouble in other cities and other provinces—East Java, Sulawesi, Madura island. The morning after the tumultuous final day of the election campaign, I flew to one of these cities, Banjarmasin in southern Borneo, where worse than usual violence had been reported the day before.

Taxi drivers at the airport were reluctant to go into town. Even on its outskirts you could smell smoke, and a Protestant church at its centre was still burning after twenty-four hours. An entire slum block had been destroyed, and the rioters had fired the offices of the ruling party, a dozen shops and cinemas and the best hotel in town. In the big shopping centre, 132 bodies were found. A police colonel from Jakarta told me that they were looters, trapped by their own fire, though others said that they were victims of the military who had been murdered elsewhere and covertly dumped in the burning building. I saw two of these bodies in the hospital mortuary. They were burned beyond recognition, their skulls cracked by the heat.

As I was preparing to leave Banjarmasin, I glanced at the map of Borneo and noticed a name in the province of West Kalimantan: Pontianak—the place where Jonathan had filmed the photograph of the severed head. Borneo is vast, and the two cities are hundreds of miles apart. But the Chinese travel agent in the hotel was enthusiastic: Pontianak was a splendid city, he explained, with a large Chinese population. He quickly fixed the flights, and gave me the telephone number of a friend who could act as my guide there.

From the plane, West Kalimantan was flat and regular, but cut through with exciting, chocolate-brown rivers. There were naked patches in the jungle, and thin lines of smoke rose from invisible fires. Through the porthole I saw metal roofs and boats, and more brown river water. Then the plane banked and I was looking at jungle again, then at an airport in the jungle.

The city below me was Pontianak (the word means evil spirit); it lies on the Equator (dead on it, according to my guidebook). Things learned about the Equator as a child came back to me, such as the way the direction of water going down the plughole reverses when you cross it. I caught myself thinking about ways of testing this—

perhaps in different hotels, one north, one south. Then the plane tilted down and began its descent towards the centre of the earth.

Two

My knowledge of Borneo was vague. I seemed to remember that it was the third biggest island in the world. I thought of jungles, of course, and of copper-engraved encounters between European explorers in canoes and cannibal chieftains. I thought of a poster which I had seen as a child, featuring a wrestler known as the Wild Man of Borneo. I found myself trying to remember if the adventures of Tintin had ever taken him there. At the airport, I bought a glossy guidebook, and recalled what I had heard in Jakarta.

In February, rumours had filtered through of fighting between two ethnic groups, the Dayaks and the Madurese. The Dayaks were the original inhabitants of the island, famous during the nineteenth century as the archetypal Victorian 'savages'. For thousands of years, before the arrival of the Dutch and the British, they dominated Borneo; they were a scattered collection of tribes who lived in communal 'longhouses', practised a form of animism, and survived by hunting, and by slash-and-burn agriculture.

More titillating, to the Victorian mind, was the promiscuity held to be rampant in these longhouses, and the practice of 'male enhancement': the piercing of the penis with a metal pin. Dayak warriors increased their prestige, and brought good luck to their villages, by collecting the heads of rival tribes in highly ritualized raids. Certain of the victims' organs, including the heart, brains and blood, were believed to bestow potency on those who consumed them, and the heads were preserved and worshipped in elaborate rituals. 'Beautiful young girls,' my guidebook informed me, 'would snatch up the heads and use the grisly trophies as props in a wild and erotic burlesque.'

The Dayaks' bloodier traditions were outlawed by the Christian colonists; since 1945 they had been full citizens of the Indonesian republic. My guidebook contained photographs of old people in beaded headdresses, and men in loincloths clutching blowpipes, but they had about them the glazed neatness of tourist entertainments. 'These days Dayaks keep their penis pins and tattoos well hidden

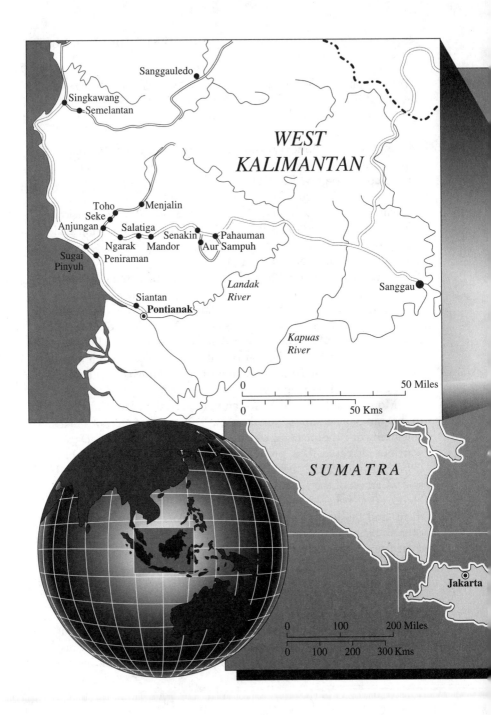

Sanggauledo

Singkawang
Semelantan

WEST
KALIMANTAN

Toho
Seke   Menjalin
Anjungan   Salatiga
Ngarak   Senakin   Pahauman
Mandor   Aur Sampuh
Sugai
Pinyuh   Peniraman

Landak
River   Sanggau

Siantan   Kapuas
Pontianak   River

0   50 Miles

0   50 Kms

SUMATRA

Jakarta

0   100   200 Miles

0   100   200   300 Kms

SUE WORTH/LYVENNET

beneath jeans and T-shirts,' I read. 'Apart from a few villages in the interior, the longhouses have been replaced by simple homes of wood and plaster.'

The Madurese, I had heard several times, were 'the Sicilians of Indonesia'; educated Jakartans smiled wearily and shook their heads when they spoke of them. Madura was a dry, barren island off the east coast of Java, the frequent beneficiary of the government's programme of subsidized 'transmigration' to the more fertile territories of the outer archipelago. Its inhabitants had a national reputation for coarseness, armed violence, and an uncompromising form of Islam. I had heard them blamed for church burnings, attacks on Christians, and several riots during the election campaign. Everywhere they settled, the Madurese had become the neighbours that nobody wanted.

As transmigrants, they were accused of thievery and thuggishness, but their differences with the Dayaks were older and ran deeper than that. The Madurese were proud bearers of curved sickles; Dayak tradition abhorred the public flaunting of blades. The Dayaks hunted and reared pigs; the Madurese were strict Muslims. Violence had been breaking out between the two groups since the first Madurese arrived in West Kalimantan early this century. But nothing had ever been seen like the events of the previous months.

I had a cutting from the *Asia Times* of 20 February 1997. It was headlined FIGHT TO THE DEATH FOR TRIBAL RIGHTS.

It's been two generations since the last reports of headhunting by the Dayak, one of the most feared tribes in Southeast Asia. Now one of Indonesia's oldest societies is running amok and returning to its brutal traditions.

The Madurese, a migrant ethnic group from the island of Madura, east of Java, are bearing the brunt of the Dayaks' anger, fuelled not only by cultural conflicts but by political and economic discontent. Following several clashes between the two groups, Madurese have watched dozens of their settlements north-east of Pontianak, the capital of West Kalimantan, burn to the ground.

The burnings and killings continue. Despite repeated government announcements that the area is safe, the Dayak and Indonesian army roadblocks still stand. There is widespread fear that violence, even in Pontianak, can break out anytime.

'This is a time bomb. It can explode at any minute,' said one Dayak.

A government estimate of a few hundred dead was cited. 'Local Christian church leaders' were said to put them 'in the thousands'. The author of the article, a Javanese woman, was a friend of Jonathan; her visit to West Kalimantan, he told me, had left her badly scared. 'At a roadblock the next day—during a three-hundred-kilometre journey my companion and I encountered thirty-two roadblocks,' she wrote, 'an old Dayak man with a rifle asked: "Are you Madurese? I want to drink some Madurese blood."'

But her article made no explicit reference to the most striking aspect of the war in West Kalimantan. For the Dayaks, it was said, had not merely driven out and killed their Madurese neighbours. They had ritually decapitated them, carried off their heads as trophies, and eaten their hearts and livers.

Jonathan had heard vague stories about the violence in February; a few days later, he flew over to Pontianak with a small group of foreign journalists based in Jakarta. They checked into the city's one good hotel, the same one to which I was heading. Its lounge, restaurant and karaoke bar were full of poorly disguised representatives of Intel, the state security organization. The next day, they hired a driver and a jeep, and drove north out of Pontianak. There were soldiers on the streets, and checkpoints every few miles with spikes and mines spread across the road. They got through the first few by waving press passes or pretending to be tourists.

At a village called Salatiga, they saw the first signs of destruction: dozens of burned, skeletal houses, 'like pictures of Bosnia', Jonathan said. They pulled over, but after the cameraman started filming some soldiers arrived, angry and nervous. Calls were made to headquarters, and the cameraman's tapes were confiscated (though a few had been hastily concealed in the jeep). Back in Pontianak, they were held for several hours and then released, with orders not to wander outside the city itself.

They spent the evening in the bar of the hotel, watching the Intel men get drunk and sing karaoke.

The next day they talked to people in Pontianak, and realized for the first time how little of the full story had reached Jakarta. There had been massacres, people said, in most of the villages in the interior. First, the Madurese had attacked the Dayaks, then the Dayaks had taken revenge. They had assembled from all over Kalimantan, ritually summoned by something called the Red Bowl. Then they had systematically purged the villages of Madurese settlers, burning their houses and hunting them down.

The Dayaks' magic made them invulnerable to bullets, people said. They could identify the Madurese by their smell. A woman from Salatiga claimed to have looked out of her window and seen a man walking down the road carrying a head impaled on a stick. A journalist on a local magazine had a photograph of a severed head— the very photograph which Jonathan had used in his film.

The Dayaks were trying to get through to Pontianak, where thousands of Madurese were living as refugees. The army was protecting the Madurese and, people said, killing Dayaks. According to the official count 300 people had died. Everyone knew that the true figure was far, far higher.

Everyone was scared of something: the Madurese of the Dayaks, the Dayaks of the army, and the army and the local government of the trouble which this was going to cause back in Jakarta. Military reinforcements had been flown in from Java, and the hospitals were under guard.

Everywhere they went, Jonathan and his friends were followed. People were afraid to talk to them. After a couple more nights of karaoke with the Intels, they flew back to Jakarta.

That was three months ago. Since then, there had been no more reports of significant trouble, and these days everyone in Jakarta was preoccupied with the election. An extraordinary thing had taken place, and passed by with no more than a glance from the outside world: just a couple of hours' drive from a modern city of banks, hotels and airports, there had been an ethnic war of scarcely imaginable savagery, fought according to principles of black magic.

Three

The morning after I arrived in Pontianak, I drove out of the city with my guide, a Chinese named Budi who always wore black shoes, black trousers and a white shirt. We crossed Pontianak's two rivers, where the seagoing schooners docked, curved and glistening like great white ice-cream scoops, and where the riverboats began the long chug to the interior. The outskirts of the town were dominated by water, and wide ditches divided the houses from the road and from one another. Bouncing planks were laid across them. Some families even kept tiny tub-like boats moored by their front doors. We passed the Equator monument, a strange black sculpture of concentric hoops, and drove north along a crisp new road unrolled like a carpet on an underlay of dusty red earth.

Budi could tell at a glance which houses were Dayak and which were Madurese, by the arrangement of the stilts, the position of the windows and the presence or absence of batik decorations above the door. His English was as precise as his clothes; he could put a date or a number to everything. As we drove north, he told me what he knew about the struggle between the Dayaks and the Madurese. He had no hesitation in calling it a war.

It had begun at the very end of last year in a town called Sanggauledo, close to the border with Malaysian Sarawak. A stage had been specially built for a live performance of *dangdut*, the bouncy, Indian-influenced pop music adored all over Indonesia. At some point during the course of the evening, two Dayak women had been bothered by a pair of Madurese boys. A fight broke out, the Madurese brandished their sickles, and a young Dayak, the son of the local village head, was stabbed. Scared and outnumbered, the Madurese took refuge in the local military outpost, where a delegation of Dayaks quickly presented themselves, demanding that the two be handed over. The soldiers refused, so they walked to the nearest Madurese enclave and set it on fire. 'Nine hundred and ninety-eight houses were burned,' Budi said. 'Some of them were completely destroyed.'

Tension between the two races had been building for years; there had been a similar spasm of violence a decade ago. But this time, when news of the stabbing spread from Sanggauledo, there was a round of revenge attacks on Madurese living in the interior. Within a few days the government in Pontianak got together a group of Dayak and Madurese leaders and drew up a 'treaty'.

Over the years the Madurese had not been the only objects of the Dayaks' fury. During the Second World War the Dayaks had been recruited by both sides in the fighting between the Japanese and the Allies. Twenty years later, they had turned on the Chinese of Kalimantan, during the great bloodletting, anti-Communist in pretext, which swept Indonesia in the mid-1960s. Budi was old enough to remember that time, but he spoke warmly of the Dayaks.

'Inside, I am pro-Dayak,' he said. 'They are good people, very gentle, they don't cause trouble for no one. They want to be left alone. But they are lazy. I have to say that they are very lazy. My brother works with Dayaks in his office, and if you leave them alone they will sit there all day talking and smiling. Their IQ is very low, unfortunately.'

Even from our brief acquaintance I knew that Budi worked from seven o'clock in the morning until midnight every day. I suspected that, to him, most people looked fairly lazy.

For an hour the jungle had been close on either side, broken up by the occasional lonely hut and wooden stands selling cigarettes and Coke. Now there were houses on both sides of the road, and suddenly we were in a small town of concrete offices and bright, dusty shop signs. Right in the centre was a spectacularly burned-out house, flanked on both sides by intact buildings. Budi was not sure what this meant. 'This town has a reputation for burning down houses,' he said. 'By accident. Maybe they are careless with matches.'

I was looking for the town's priests, friends of an anthropologist in Pontianak and witnesses, I was told, to much of the worst violence. On the outskirts, we followed a trail of schoolchildren to a tin-roofed church and a school, built of flaking planks on low stilts, which stood back from the road. Close to these buildings was the house of Father Anselmus and Father Andreas.

They were young priests, Dayaks in their late twenties, who had studied at a Catholic seminary in Java. But apart from a crucifix nailed to one wall there was nothing priestly about their bungalow. The main room contained a shelf of novels, a table of ashtrays and discarded fruit-peel, and a wide TV wired to a satellite dish on the roof. On the walls were a painting of a volcano, a Dayak shield and scabbard, and a marker board, which was filled with a scrawled list of dates and appointments in Indonesian and the following words in English: DON'T FORGET TO SHOW THE CHAMPION'S FINAL ON THURSDAY, MAY 28 (DAWN) BORUSSIA DORTMUND VS. JUVENTUS!

Next to the board was a five-foot-high cut-out of Father Christmas.

Andreas was bearded and sleepy-eyed, with a dazed kind of grin. He smoked lots of *kreteks*—Indonesian clove cigarettes—which he held between three fingers, as if unsure what to make of them. Anselmus was taller and more talkative, and gave the impression of being a bit too muscular and handsome for this kind of life.

They were the first Dayaks I had encountered and I expected to be met with wariness and reserve—in the car, Budi and I had rehearsed a reassuring preamble which emphasized the seriousness of my intentions, and the confidentiality with which any information would be treated. It was quite unnecessary with these two, who reminded me more than anything of certain friends in London, aimless, well-meaning bachelors resigned to the light duties of dole-claiming, TV-watching and smoking. They welcomed us immediately; there was always coffee and fruit on the table, and after a few days it became natural, almost routine, to drop round at Anselmus and Andreas's house for durian or rambutan and a conversation about headhunting and cannibalism.

They took up the story where Budi had left off. The 'peace treaty' had been signed by the Dayak and Madurese leaders in mid-January, but even before the end of the month the violence had begun again. On 29 January news spread of two Dayak girls, former pupils at Anselm and Andreas's school, who had been lying in bed in Siantan, a suburb north of Pontianak, when two Madurese men broke in. The girls were molested; their nightdresses were cut with sickles. Anticipating another round of revenge attacks, a mob of Madurese gathered in the centre of Sungai Pinyuh, on the road between Pontianak and the Dayak interior.

By four o'clock in the afternoon, 1,000 people armed with sickles had assembled, old men and children among them. But no Dayaks appeared. The mob grew impatient and burned down a

Dayak house. Then they began stopping cars and demanding to see the occupants' papers.

They set up a roadblock in Peniraman, another town on the main road where a family was driving back from a daughter's university graduation ceremony. Their jeep was stopped and the five occupants were dragged out. All but a child and a young woman were cut down on the spot. Andreas himself had conducted the funeral of a young man named Alun, whose head had been almost severed by the sickles. The body of an old man, a village elder named Nyuncat, was found later in the jungle.

Word of the atrocities passed around the Dayak villages; and the Madurese, convinced that retaliation was imminent, stepped up their slaughter. It was said that the Dayaks were 'passing the Red Bowl'—some kind of symbolic call to arms. On 29 January half a dozen Dayak houses had been burned in Senakin. On the following morning, the Madurese in Paci Karangan were attacked by Dayaks. That afternoon, Madurese threw stones at a Dayak bus in Seke. The next day, Andreas saw Dayaks burning down Madurese houses in Seke which had already been abandoned.

'In the afternoon, in Paci, I saw dead bodies on the road without heads and without hearts,' said Andreas. Both the priests had thin smiles on their faces, and the more details I pressed out of them, the wider the smiles became.

'What had happened to them?' I asked through Budi.

'Some Dayak people killed them and cut their heads off.' Smile.

'What did they do with the heads?'

'The heads they took away.' Grin. 'The bodies were all empty. Near the body were the stomach and the insides. They were there for a long time. None of the pastors was brave enough to perform the burials for a month.'

'It must have been terrible, seeing the bodies there.'

'This was my first time to see a body without a head and, as a pastor, it was terrible. It was as if everything I have been teaching has had no effect at all.' Anselm nodded in agreement, and they looked at one another and smiled again. They smiled widely, their straggly moustaches crinkled and lifted. They laughed out loud in dismay and puzzlement.

It was four o'clock by the time we left the pastors; the shadows were thickening as we drove on past a military barracks with painted signs in front bearing divisional crests.

When the trouble began at the end of January, the smaller military outposts beyond here had quickly lost control and, having cleared the villages of the interior, the Dayaks had moved towards Pontianak. But the army mustered its forces; troops were brought in from other parts of Indonesia. At a town called Anjungan the Dayaks were stopped by force, and there were stories that bus-loads of Dayak men had been massacred by the soldiers.

The gateways to the barracks bore the numbers 17.8.45— Independence Day—and the gold eagle of the Republic of Indonesia, hunched and stylized like the Roman eagle. It was easy to think of these soldiers as Roman legionaries, gathered up from Java, from Sulawesi or Bali, and forced to do their time in this outpost of the Empire, marooned among equatorial Picts and Huns, people with strange ways who wished them no good.

When my friends from Jakarta had come here there had been roadblocks and landmines, and soldiers stepping out of the jungle. But this evening there were only dogs skulking at the roadside, and vendors of cigarettes and chewing gum, who were beginning to switch on the feeble electric bulbs which lit their stalls. In a way I was childishly disappointed. When a soldier flagged us down, we tensed. But all he wanted was a lift, and we were going in the wrong direction. We passed a marshy lake. Low hills rose in the distance. Girls could be seen bathing in the river below a bridge. The road narrowed and a tunnel of trees joined arms above our heads, casting stripes of shadow across the road as the sun declined on our left.

Then, at a point difficult to define, we crossed Dayak lines.

The first sign was a burned-out house. Then there was another one, a few yards back from the road, just black beams and twists of corrugated iron. The third ruin had retained three of its pillars, so that it looked almost classical. Next to it was a house with half of its front wall intact. Budi slowed and translated the words scraped on it with charcoal. MADURESE OFFSPRING OF DOGS.

Four, five, six burned houses so far, in the space of a few hundred yards. Then twelve, thirteen and probably more behind, shrouded by the dusk and jungle. I counted fifteen in the course of about a mile, and then suddenly we were back in a village again. There was a wooden chapel and a shop selling baskets and jerrycans.

People in shorts, most of them young, walked up and down the road, or squatted with cigarettes on the verges. The houses were plaster and a few of them supported big grey satellite dishes. There was a church, but no mosque, and a soccer game was in progress on a patch of rough ground. The black ruins seemed like a hallucination.

Budi did not slow down. We passed through and drove into the jungle again.

The light ebbed away. The headlights picked out a man's jacket, carefully spreadeagled on the road ahead. 'Some accident, I suppose,' said Budi and, sure enough, around the next curve a minibus lay neatly on its side with its wheels above the roadside ditch. It was hard to tell when the accident had happened—it could have been hours ago. There were about a dozen people around the bus, apparently its passengers, though they looked unhurt and unsurprised. The men were standing with cigarettes in their hands. The women were laughing and talking, seated on a stack of chests and suitcases which, lashed to the roof, must have contributed to the bus's instability. 'You have to be careful driving here,' said Budi. 'Animals come out of the jungle. Dayak people walk straight out into the road. They are kind people, but they are vague. Sometimes you stop and ask directions. They say, "It's not far," but then you drive a long way and still don't get there. And these people walk it—they walk for kilometres and kilometres, but still they say when you ask them, "It's not far."'

Later, Budi said: 'You don't see them from the road, but a lot of people live there, inside the jungle. People die here quite often, outside of the statistics. They just die and nobody knows about them.' When we drove back along the same road, four hours later, the luggage, the bus and its passengers were still there, smiling and smoking in the darkness.

Four

It was before six, but it felt very late by the time we reached Menjalin, another plaster-and-satellite-dish village, where teenagers sat in open doorways under dim flickering bulbs. They smiled at Budi, and jumped up to offer help when he stopped for directions. In the middle of the village was a large wooden house where a group of figures were arrayed in an unconsciously picturesque composition. A dozen Dayak boys were lying or sitting on the veranda, and at their centre was an old man with spectacles and a white beard, a portly old white man with a tin of rolling tobacco on his knee, gesturing and talking as the boys looked up at him.

His name was Father Kristof, and he was a Dutch Capuchin priest. He had been in Indonesia for thirty-one years, and in Menjalin for sixteen. There was a Swiss priest in Ngarak, and another Dutchman in Singkawang, but foreigners here were few and he said without regret that he didn't get many visitors. He wore a fake Calvin Klein T-shirt, but the room where he led us was dark and timeless, with a stone floor, a wooden dining table and a shelf of books with cracked leather spines. He understood English and spoke it with a strong accent, but the effort made him frown and, after nodding at my questions, he would direct the answers at Budi in Indonesian, and correct the translation as it was relayed back to me.

Menjalin had been tense since the New Year. When the news came through of the Madurese attacks on the schoolgirls and the motorists, some kind of reaction had been inevitable.

'It was not unexpected,' said Father Kristof. 'But it was very sudden. People from all walks of life, even children, gathered outside. They were unanimous, they decided as a community to fight for their rights. Everyone wanted to go—even my friends, these boys outside, they made bamboo spears, they carried knives. They marched to Seke and Salatiga. They said that they must defend themselves. They say that the Madurese have killed Dayaks so very, very many times but this is enough. All Madurese must leave Kalimantan.'

It was a collective decision, he kept emphasizing: there was no leader. It was entirely spontaneous. But it did sound well organized. All the participants abided strictly by three rules. First, they would not damage any mosques. Second, they would not burn down any state-owned offices. 'Now this is very wise,' he said, 'because if they burn mosques, then they are Christians against Muslims...' He fixed me with his eye and shook his head, as if to stress what the consequences of this would have been, how close they had come to a holy war. 'If they damage government property, they are against the government, and nobody can defeat the government.' The third rule was no looting. 'They are not rich people, but when they found cars or nice furniture, they burned them.'

Since the trouble at the pop concert, Dayaks all over West Kalimantan had been preparing. When fighting began in December they had only sharpened bamboo poles and a few hunting rifles. A month later they had metal heads for the spears, and newly forged *mandau*, the traditional hacking machete. They had rifles, bought illegally from the Indonesian army, smuggled across the border from Malaysia, or made out of metal tubing by local blacksmiths. Father Kristof passed an album of photographs which showed the Menjalin Dayaks preparing for battle. They had feathers tied to their heads with red ribbons, and ribbons on their spears. Their mouths were strangely synchronized: all closed, or simultaneously open in a pursed O. 'You can see from their faces that they are in a trance,' said Father Kristof. 'Individual responsibility is very, very little from person to person.'

I asked about magic, and the stories I had heard of Dayaks who were invulnerable to bullets.

'There is a lot of truth there,' said the pastor. 'If they believe that they are bulletproof, they become bulletproof. This power varies.' The priest claimed to have personally witnessed one such magical incident. A Dayak man had been shot at by a Madurese rifle. The bullet had entered his ear, and then stopped. 'He reached in,'—Father Kristof mimed the action—'and pulled it out.' In a trance, a man could walk through the jungle for hours, without eating or drinking, and without any fatigue. 'Twenty-five or thirty kilometres they go, to Salatiga and then back again. Sixty kilometres on foot, they run there and back, and they don't even drink water. When the *kamang tariu* are inside a person they scream and yell. When they return they have almost no voice left. But they can do these things because they are not themselves, because they are in a trance.'

The *kamang tariu* is the spirit which possesses the Dayaks in time of war. When it is present, it provides physical protection and immunity from thirst and fatigue, but it has a powerful appetite of its own. 'The *kamang tariu* drinks blood, it has to be fed blood,' said the pastor. 'There were Dayaks in Pontianak who could not go to the war, but who were possessed by the *tariu*. Their friends had to cut the throat of a chicken and give it to them, to feed the spirit.'

I asked what happened when the Dayaks returned from an attack on a village.

'They bring back bags of heads. The heart, they eat directly. The idea is that it should be still fresh. A fresh heart has different power from lungs, and lungs are different from stomachs. Even the blood. From children to old people to babies, no exceptions at all. Four thousand of them, all beheaded with *mandau*. Yes, it is remarkable.'

For two weeks, there was an atmosphere of emergency. Having purged the villages of the interior, the Dayaks were attempting to reach Pontianak to do the same. It seemed remarkable, given the punishment which they had inflicted on their enemies, but they felt themselves to be the ones in acute peril. 'It was very dangerous,' said Father Kristof. 'There were a lot of Madurese hiding in the bush, and people were afraid that they would come back and take their revenge.' Beyond Anjungan, the small military outposts were separated from one another by hours of road and miles of jungle. Central control had broken down completely.

Eventually, military reinforcements were flown in, and the roads were blocked by tyre spikes and mines. The soldiers went into the jungle and laid booby traps along the tracks, consisting of hand grenades and tripwires. It was now that Dayaks began to die. 'I would say that fewer than two hundred Dayak people were killed, and roughly four thousand Madurese,' said Father Kristof. 'Two thousand is sure. This is the information we have today.'

Having stopped the killing, the government in Pontianak did what it always did after this kind of trouble. It held a peace ceremony.

The authorities were sophisticated enough to know that ending the killing would not be enough to bring about peace. They recognized the magical aspects of the conflict, and knew that to control the situation on the ground they had to control the spirits. They knew about the two kinds of spirit, the *kamang*, the protector of the headhunters, and the *sumangat*, the spirit of life. In time of war, the *sumangat* flee the hearts of the people to make way for the *kamang.* So they assembled a group of compliant Dayak elders, who summoned the peaceful spirits back.

'During the government's ceremony they called back all the *sumangat*, which are harmony, peace, the spirit of life,' said Father Kristof. 'But the *kamang tariu* has not gone away. They called back the spirit of life, without sending the spirit of war back to the mountain.' This was a theological impossibility, as the old men who performed the ceremony must have known. Only the civil servants in Pontianak believed that the spirits of killing had gone. 'The government ceremony was a nonsense,' said Father Kristof.

While we were talking, the lights cut out in the stone-floored room. The noises of the jungle rose up from behind the house: the shimmering cheeps and kackacks of invisible insects, the shiver of the trees. For a few seconds we were held in darkness. Then the generator restarted its whirring.

I blinked and said, 'Father, as a priest, how do you see all this?'

'It's difficult to say in two or three words, but to understand you have to go back sixteen years to when I arrived here. Compared to then, all the Dayaks are now Christians. They go to war with a cross. They've all bought rosaries. They are not killers.' And then, in English: 'It's very difficult to explain...

'Those involved in the war didn't want any of it. They did it against their will. They didn't intend to do anything wrong. They did it all unconsciously. Even if they killed four thousand people, they are not the killers of the Madurese.

'Dayaks have two sets of rules and teachings—the ones of their ancestors, and the rules and regulations set by the government. But when they are under pressure and need to express what they are all feeling in the face of that pressure, they have no choice. They have to go by the ancestral book.'

I asked where the Bible fitted into this.

'It's hard to say. Maybe those involved in the situation, deep in a trance based on the teachings of their ancestors, poorly educated...' He shook his head, and began another train of thought. 'The educated ones didn't get involved—they refused that kind of belief...'

I asked: 'Is it a sin to cut the heads off Madurese?'

'I cannot see into people's souls,' said Father Kristof. 'I can only see their actions and here I can see that they act together, not on their own, that they act because they believe it is a good thing. I say in church it is wrong to murder, you must save the life of every person living on earth and they understand that, but when it is war...there are other things.'

'Did you try to persuade them not to go?'

'Oh, yah, but it was not possible. They laughed at it.' There was a long pause. I could hear the insects even above the hum of the generator.

Finally, Father Kristof said, 'When we love people—' then stopped, then started again. 'If a son commits murder and goes to prison, the mother always loves him. She says, "My son is a good boy still." I don't say that what has happened here is good. You have to try to understand the position of the Dayak people now.

'They are ignored by the government. They have no political role. No one in the key positions, no people of influence in the army. They are under pressure and they have no economic power. All they have is land—land that has been theirs for thousands of years. Now the government appropriates the land for transmigration. The timber companies come, other commercial concerns. The Dayaks become upset, alienated from society. That's what makes them stand up for their rights. They are'—he struggled for the right word, back in English again now—'natural people. They are in conflict with a tribe that has totally different traditions.

'It is one thing, one thing inspired it all: powerlessness. They are ignored by the government, but pressured and punished at the same time. The only way out was to do what they did.'

'These heads, Father, which they brought back from Salatiga. Where are they now?'

'They are in the villages. They bring them back into their homes, and usually perform some kind of charms or prayers. In the old days, they kept the head in a special place in the longhouse but now they keep it in a hidden place, a secret place where they pray.'

'Would they show them to you?'

'They would if I asked.'

'Would they show me?'

He did not smile, but tilted his head and looked at me. 'No. Not in this situation. It's impossible for many reasons. Because of…protocol, and because they believe the magic power will be lost.'

Later, as we were leaving, Father Kristof led us to the back of the house and a crude wooden shed on the very edge of the jungle. Inside were tables and upright boards bearing dozens of black-and-white photographs, pre-war shots of Dayaks and Dutch Fathers, praying together, standing stiffly at a harvest celebration alongside bales of rice and the carcasses of hogs. One picture dated from 1935. In it a Father, portly and bearded like Kristof, sat in a wooden chair beneath a string of nine enemy heads. The expression on his face gave nothing away. On the cheeks of the decapitated warriors, I could still make out the tattoos.

Five

'When you are accustomed to using scientific means of investigation, your mind shies away from these things,' a Dayak anthropologist said to me in Pontianak. 'But I believe there is a supernatural world. I have to believe it, because I have heard about it from soldiers, policemen, Dayak elders, Chinese, Malays. It is hard to disbelieve these people, but it is also hard to believe them.'

Everyone I met in West Kalimantan had tales of Dayak magic. I heard early on about the *panglima*, the 'generals' or war magicians who lead the Dayaks in times of emergency. I was told how a *panglima* had summoned bees to attack the Indonesian soldiers, and how he could fly, or take the form of a dog, and behead his enemies with the stroke of a leaf from a certain tree. How a pair of army officers in the north died vomiting blood after a curse was placed upon them, and how the psychiatric wards were filled with soldiers unhinged by what they had seen. 'I've talked to soldiers who have served in East Timor, and Irian Jaya,' said Father Andreas. 'They are tough men. They have killed and been shot at before, but they say that they have never been more scared than they were by the Dayak people.'

In Sanggau, a river city deep in the interior, a small group of Dayaks was crying for the blood of six Madurese who were under guard in a small military outpost. The soldiers kept them at bay, the story went, until the *panglima* arrived at the head of an army of thousands of warriors. The soldiers were not fools; a few of them were Dayaks themselves. They handed over the doomed Madurese and surrendered.

But the *panglima* was alone; there was no Dayak army. The warriors at his side were the *kamang*, the spirits of war and killing, made visible in the minds of the soldiers by the general's incantation.

At the house of the young priests, Father Anselmus showed me the collection of magical objects given to him by his parishioners. There was a cracked plastic bottle containing a few inches of oily black liquid. 'Poison,' he said with a grin. 'They put it on the edge of the *mandau*, or the blowpipe arrows. Even if you just have a cut or a scratch and it gets on your skin, you'll be dead in five minutes.' On the plastic bottle were the printed words: METRO FACE TONIC.

There was a bag of dried roots and tubers for use against the same poison, and a black stone which soothed stings and bites. There was also a matchbox filled with pieces of a dried leaf, a couple of shreds of which ensured protection from the blows of the *mandau*. 'The leaf is very rare,' said Anselm. 'They find where it is growing in their dreams. When someone has eaten *this*, the only thing which can kill them is *this*.' He presented a spear sharply whittled out of a pale, unbending wood. 'Since this war began, there's been a lot of interest in black magic.'

Andreas nodded his head and smiled. 'A man once came to me and said, "Father, why do you pray so hard for things which never come true? When we pray to the evil spirits, our wishes are fulfilled."'

A taxi driver told me another story about a Dayak who, alone of his companions, had made it to the town without being shot, captured or killed by booby traps in the jungle. Finally he fell into the hands of a group of Madurese, who pinned him down and stabbed him repeatedly. But the blows had no effect. They kicked his head until his nose hung loose and his lips were shredded, but he still looked them in the eye. It was only when they held his face under in a basin of water that he stopped moving.

It was not easy to find people who had witnessed such things first-hand.

One man, a Dayak schoolmaster in a village which saw one of the worst battles, described to me the most widely known manifestation of Dayak magic, the invulnerability to bullets. 'In my town, there were only three soldiers,' he said, 'and when the Dayaks first arrived they fired into the air. But they were completely outnumbered, and soon began shooting straight into them. There was one Dayak, he was thirty yards away. The soldier aimed the gun, it went "Bang-bang!", but it didn't hurt him. They were firing to kill, but none of the Dayaks got shot. I'd heard about it, but until then I never believed it. When they are in that state, when they are filled with the spirits, nothing can harm them.'

I went to see a man named Miden, a *timanggong* or tribal elder, in a hamlet called Aur Sampuh. He was small and alert, the picture of respectability in an ironed shirt and cream trousers, and his neat, cool house was a centre of village activity. On the wall were two carved Dayak shields, and a calendar in the yellow colours of the Indonesian ruling party. Snake tattoos ran down his arms and on to the back of his hands.

He began by explaining the animistic principles of Dayak religion. Spirits reside in everything, and it is the duty of Dayaks to acknowledge and propitiate these spirits at each stage of the farming cycle. 'When we cut down a tree we have to show the tree's spirit that we only do it to make our living. When we plant rice, we sing a song. When the rice grows to a certain height there is a ceremony; there is another ceremony to thank the gods at harvest time.'

As a *timanggong*, Miden performed marriages, christenings and funerals. There were rituals to purify the paddies and keep away birds, 'but I am a farmer as well as a priest. I also use pesticides.' I asked him how he had become a Dayak priest. 'When I was a child I followed the *timanggong* in the village, and I learned much.' As well as keeping their own religion, the Dayaks in this village were all Christians, most of them Catholics.

I asked about the trouble in January and February. He said that there had been none in Aur Sampuh because there were no Madurese here, and therefore no grievance. It was a little frustrating talking to him, and I felt as if there were two sides to Pak (Mr) Miden: the *timanggong* with his ritual knowledge, and the local politician with the ruling party's calendar on his wall. Whenever the former was about to say something interesting, the latter always butted in with vague, conciliatory politeness.

He spoke with authority of the Dayak war rituals, but always in the abstract, as something from which he had been entirely removed. The fighting had stranded him in his village—for two months he had been unable to leave Aur Sampuh, he said, in a way that made it sound like an isolated island rather than a small village less than an hour from some of the worst killing.

'What is the Red Bowl?' I asked.

'The Red Bowl is used to call people. It's a symbol of communication used during times of emergency. When a messenger carries it from one tribe to the next it means, "Come and help us."'

Each tribe, he said, has its own bowl—it was red with blood and decorated with chicken feathers. If a *timanggong* received the Red Bowl then he was obliged to send at least seven warriors to help his brothers. It passed from village to village—during the Japanese occupation, and in 1967 when the government was fighting the Chinese 'communists', every village received the Red Bowl. 'Compared to then, this was not a big war,' Pak Miden said emphatically. 'I am very glad that this village did not receive the Red Bowl.'

One of the mysteries of the killings in January and February was how quickly the Dayaks mobilized and the coordination they displayed across a large area with poor roads and few telephones. If the warring parties did have ringleaders, they had not been publicly identified, and Miden insisted that the ceremonies were conducted spontaneously, and that he himself would never have anything to do with the summoning of the war spirits.

'If a *timanggong* knows that they are going to hold this ritual, he will forbid it.' There was, he supposed, someone who 'coordinated' the ceremony. He did not know who it was.

I asked him about the nature of the mysterious 'generals', the *panglima*. My impression had been that nobody knew who they were, that they lived in the mountains as hermits, halfway to being spirits themselves, and that they appeared mysteriously in the villages at just the right moment. Pak Miden confirmed that the *panglima* could not be killed, and that they could sniff out Madurese and tell them apart from Malays and Javanese. But a *panglima* was a man, and he could be any man; until the summoning began no one could tell whom the spirits would choose. 'The *panglima* could be a different person every time,' he said. 'He is whoever is the strongest of the Dayaks.'

In other words, there were no ringleaders, no decision-making process and no responsibility. The Dayaks had been provoked, and gathered together to hold a ceremony. With that decision they had surrendered their free will to the spirits.

Later I read an article on this subject by Stephanus Djuweng, the director of the Institute of Dayakology Research and Development in Pontianak. He took as his starting point the architecture of the traditional Dayak longhouse, of which a handful survive in use. The old longhouses contained family apartments called *bilek* which gave on to a communal area called the *soah*. 'Each *bilek* is owned by an individual,' he wrote, 'whereas each *soah* is a collective part of the longhouse. This type of architectural pattern symbolizes the balance between individual and collective rights.'

It is an attractive analogy, particularly useful, as Djuweng pointed out, for a country like Indonesia, a sprawling archipelagic empire of hundreds of different races and languages. 'The Dayak are normal human beings. They will protect themselves if any of their ancestral lands or property rights are violated, or if community members are treated beyond the limits of tolerance,' Djuweng said. But earlier in the same article he had put it rather differently. 'What honey bees,' he asked, 'would not defend themselves when their honey, nests and community members are threatened?'

Six

Every day for a week, Budi and I drove up and down the road that led to the interior, past burned-out houses with jungle grass rising up through the ashes. It was three months since they had been destroyed, but most of the ruins were undisturbed, and you could still discern the outline of individual rooms beneath the twists of corrugated iron—a tin bathtub here, there a nest of forks and spoons, fused together in what must have been a kitchen.

The people we spoke to on the way knew exactly what had happened and were happy to talk about it.

In Pahauman, the man who sold us bottles of Coca-Cola described the altars which people built along the road in front of their houses. They had decorated them with severed heads. 'Less than ten,' he said, when I asked him how many heads he had seen. 'There was nobody I knew well.'

His wife said that there had been hundreds of Madurese living here before, and that she had never had any trouble with them. 'Some of them escaped to Pontianak, I suppose, but not very many probably,' she said. What did she feel about what had happened, we asked. 'Oh, it's terrible,' she said, rather cheerfully. 'I was afraid.'

In Salatiga, a man wearing a T-shirt with the logo of the government teachers' union approached us giggling. 'I speek Indonesia!' he spluttered. 'I do not speek Inggris!' He was a local Malay with a dark complexion, and with great hilarity he related the story of how the Dayak warriors had entered his house and held a knife to his throat. '"You're Madurese, you're Madurese!" they say,'—with the palm of his hand he mimed the *mandau* blade at his neck—'I say, "No, no, I'm Malay, I'm Malay!" So they ask someone in the village who knows me, and they say'—pause for dramatic effect—'"It's OK! He's *not* Madurese!" Ha ha ha ha hah!'

On the third day, Father Anselmus agreed to accompany us on the road to the interior. He would introduce us to 'key people', he said, who knew a lot about what had happened. Before we left, Andreas—who had clearly been thinking things over—talked about what he had seen during the first round of killings over the New Year.

His family home was north of Pontianak, and he had been near Sanggauledo when the first trouble began there. On 31 December, he saw the Dayaks arriving from the interior and burning the Madurese houses. On New Year's Day, he was in the town square when a crowd of 1,000 Dayaks returned from one of their expeditions. 'They were wailing like Indians in a Western, "Whoo-woo-woo-woo". One of them was carrying a head, and another guy came up to me holding something that looked like a piece of tongue. He said, "This is a heart," and raised it to his mouth and started eating it in front of my face.' Andreas mimicked the action of someone ripping a lump out of a piece of meat. 'It was dark red, but there wasn't a lot of blood on it. It wasn't fresh.' His droopy grin was wider than ever.

The first of Anselmus's key people was a prominent Dayak from Salatiga, which used to have one of the largest Madurese populations. We went to see him at his gold mine, which lay on a huge naked expanse of white sand that suddenly bared itself out of the jungle at the end of a dusty track. It was like a cartoonist's rendering of archetypal desert: undulating sand dunes dotted with the skulls of animals. The mine consisted of a large open pit into which water was trickling through blue rubber tubes. Five boys in headscarves splashed around up to their necks, breaking up the sandy sides of the pond to enrich the mud, which was sucked out by pump through a Heath Robinson construction of bamboo pipes. At the end of the pipes, it trickled over a zigzagging arrangement of wooden steps which were covered with thick sacking. It was in this sacking, if he was lucky, that Sabdi, our miner, would find grains of gold.

He had found none for a week. We sat under an improvised tent, where young men in flip-flops fiddled with oily pieces of dismantled machinery. Sabdi lived on the main road of Salatiga. The houses opposite had been owned by Madurese. On 30 January, they had responded to the rumours about the trouble in Pontianak by taking up their guns and harassing Dayak motorists. Sabdi took his family to stay with friends in the next town, and then came back himself. On 1 February, five Dayak houses were burned early in the morning. 'I saw clearly what happened,' he said.

Within a few hours, Dayaks started arriving from out of town. The Madurese were soon outnumbered and began making their escape into the jungle, but about fifty of them stayed behind and found themselves facing 1,000 Dayaks. 'Three of them got shot,' said Sabdi. 'Sinem, Haji Marsuli and another man I didn't know well. The Dayaks took the bodies and cut their heads off with *mandau*. Then they cut open their backs and pulled out the hearts, and they ate the hearts and drank the blood.'

The rest of the Madurese fled. Their houses were burned down and some of the occupants burned to death inside them. The Dayaks followed the fugitives into the jungle. 'Within a week they had killed everyone hiding in the forest,' said Sabdi. 'A couple of days later, I saw about twenty bodies of Madurese on the roadside. They didn't have heads or hearts.' About five of them were children.

Of all the Dayaks I met, Sabdi appeared to be the most troubled by what he had seen, the least susceptible to the glassy grin which spread so reliably over the faces of those who talked about severed heads and decapitated children. 'Yes, I'm glad that the Madurese have gone,' he said, 'because as long as they were here they never stopped fighting. When I saw the bodies, to be honest I felt nothing, as long as they were people I didn't know. But Sinem was my neighbour and my very good friend. I felt sad to see him shot, to see his heart cut out from behind.'

This strange and confused answer comforted me at the time. But when we were back in the jeep, Anselmus smiled at me and asked me what I had made of Sabdi. I said that he was intelligent and precise, a good witness, and Anselmus smiled again. He had run into Sabdi himself, he explained, just after the incident that had been described to us. After the rout of the Madurese, Sabdi had left Salatiga to rejoin his family in the next town where Anselmus also happened to be. The priest had met him as he arrived, and Sabdi's mouth and face had been wet with fresh blood. 'He ate somebody's heart,' smiled Anselmus. 'Maybe he had to do it, so that they would let him leave Salatiga. But it looked to me as if he was in a trance too. He did not know what he had been doing.'

Nobody we spoke to ever owned up to any personal part in the killings.

Every morning I drove with Budi past the black monument marking the centre of the earth. Our day was spent in the northern hemisphere, talking to people in the Dayak villages; every evening I went back across the Equator to my hotel in the south.

One day in Salatiga a man said, 'Would you like to see the Madurese in the jungle?'

We were sitting in a little restaurant, a concrete room covered with a rusty iron roof, eating big bowls of pork noodle soup. The soup was steaming hot and made us sweat. The man we were talking

to was another Dayak leader. He seasoned his soup elaborately with several different kinds of fierce spice. He sent for his teenage son, who arrived on a scooter and climbed into the jeep with Budi and me.

We pulled up in front of a group of a dozen burned-out houses on the edge of the village. In front of them was a bus stop with graffiti which said THANK YOU FOR GOING BACK TO MADURA ISLAND. We walked towards the jungle, past a mosque. It was deserted, and there was a litter of leaves and broken coconuts in the covered courtyard, but otherwise it was unspoiled. The forest rose up like a wall at the edge of the clearing and, on the far side of the wall, the keening of the insects became suddenly deafening. It was like being inside a huge, violently electrical machine.

We were walking along a thin track, encroached on at both sides by ferns and jungle grasses. Every few yards there would be a rubber tree with a bright gash of white sap running down the trunk into a cup of leaves. Our guide stopped every now and then to check on one. Behind him walked Budi and then me.

I found myself thinking about tripwires and hand grenades.

We turned off the track into the thicket. The young rubber-tapper hacked a path for us with his blade. He seemed to have turned off the track at random. How did he know that this was the place to make the turning? We were five minutes from the road, but I no longer knew which direction it was, and when Budi spoke to him, he just smiled vacantly at us and kept hacking. I began making calculations, such as: would a booby trap be laid so as to kill the person who triggered it, the person at the front? Or would the hand grenade be a few yards behind the tripwire, say where I was now stepping? And would Budi and I be able to overpower this boy if he turned on us? He was a foot shorter than me and skinny, but he had a *mandau*. The vegetation was a yard above my head. I could taste the pork soup in my mouth.

Someone called out from within the jungle, and our guide responded with a laugh. Out of the innards of the jungle, another boy appeared, and the two friends greeted one another. The first boy pointed towards us, as if making an introduction, and the newcomer smiled. He was young and poor and friendly, a skinny Dayak with a machete. But I had lost faith in my ability to read people's smiles.

I nodded back and asked Budi what they were saying. 'I don't know,' he said. 'They are speaking the Dayak language.'

Ten yards further on both boys stopped and pointed with their *mandau*. There, sticking out of the sludge of the jungle floor, was a skeleton.

It was half buried in leaves and sodden clothes, but it was immediately obvious that it was human. Its bright white bones made me think of specimens in school biology labs.

Two hundred yards away there were five more skeletons.

All of them were women. You could tell from their clothes, cheap artificial fibres in gaudy colours which even the jungle could not digest. In three months, the shuffling action of insects and vegetation had cleaned every scrap of flesh off their bones. Here was a line of delicate vertebrae, here a shoulder, here a nest of curved ribs. There was no smell, other than that of the earth and the leaves. None of the skeletons had skulls.

There was a child's purse, empty, with a pattern of yellow kittens. There were patterned nylon shorts, and underwear, with pelvises inside. Suddenly our guides no longer seemed remotely like potential muggers capable of murdering and robbing us; they seemed what they were, undernourished teenagers doing us a favour. We asked them what had happened to the heads of the six women.

'From when we first saw them here, they had no heads and no hearts.'

A few minutes' hack away, amid another soup of muddy clothes, there were two skulls. They were adult, but close by there was a pair of elasticated baby's knickers. The boys said that two weeks after the killings, soldiers had come here and poured petrol on the skulls and burned the remaining flesh off them.

I tried to imagine the circumstances in which these women had died.

They had fled into the jungle with their children, just as a precaution perhaps, until their men could sort out the trouble in town. From here they would have heard the shots and smelled the smoke of their houses burning. Had they understood what had happened when no help came? Perhaps the braver ones among them had walked back into Salatiga to have a look, and never returned.

115

How many nights did they spend waiting in the jungle? Did they hear the *Whoo-woo-woo-woo* and know they were being hunted? Did they know the Dayaks who killed them? Did they think (as I was thinking): *this is a joke. You don't cut people's heads off any more.* Or perhaps they understood it very well.

Five of them had died on this spot; the sixth one had died alone. Had she escaped, or fallen quite separately in an earlier encounter? They were killed by men, no doubt, who cut off their heads and ate their hearts, but they were not violated and nor was the mosque where their husbands prayed. Now they were like their houses, ruined but undisturbed by the side of the road, ignored except by curious visitors, while the grass rose up through their ribs to hide their bones.

Budi wanted to take a vertebra away as a souvenir, but I made him put it back. We walked back to the road.

We shook hands with the rubber-tappers. I felt guilty and ridiculous for having suspected them of leading us into a trap. We offered to drop them back in town, but they preferred to walk. I tried to give them money, but they refused to take it.

On the way back to Pontianak we dropped in at Andreas and Anselmus's house. The man waiting for us was the most frightened of all the people I met in Borneo.

For several days, the two priests had been trying to persuade him to meet me, but from the moment we walked through the door, he seemed to regret the decision. He sat on the far side of the fruit-peel-strewn table and nodded nervously as Anselmus explained to Budi the strict conditions on which he would talk to me. In anything I wrote, his identity must be masked completely. I promised that I would obscure not just his real name, but his profession, his age, his ethnic origin and even his appearance. Later, when he had relaxed, I began as a tease to haggle with him over this, and won the right to the following details. He was Indonesian (but not Dayak), he was in his late twenties, and he had a thin moustache and a digital watch. The day before I left Pontianak, Budi rang to say that the man had called to inform us of the pseudonym by which he wished to be known: Bernard.

Bernard lived locally, and he had something to show us, in a brown envelope which he pushed across the table.

The envelope contained photographs.

The first few showed burned-out houses, some with smoke still rising from them. On 7 February, a week after the trouble broke, Bernard had driven east towards the interior, shooting two rolls of film along the way.

The pictures showed roadblocks made of upturned tables, with slogans daubed in red on sheets of plywood.

MADURESE, CRIMINALS OF WEST KALIMANTAN.

SALATIGA WON'T TAKE MADURESE ANY MORE.

GET THE HELL BACK TO MADURA.

In Senakin, Bernard had arrived in the middle of a Dayak rally. The photographs showed a crowd of a few hundred. They were wearing T-shirts and jeans. They were carrying rifles and *mandau*, and there were feathers tied to their heads with red ribbons, and ribbons on their spears. They held banners bearing anti-Madurese slogans. In one photograph, the crowd held its arms aloft, as if punching the air. In another, the mouths of the Dayaks were open, as if shouting aloud. Behind them you could see the green hills. A group of men stood on the roof of a white bus.

'This was the first time that I felt afraid,' said Bernard.

The Dayaks were from the interior. The men on the bus were members of the regional assembly, sent to calm them down. They were visibly failing to achieve this. 'The Dayaks were all ready for war, and they were possessed, they weren't acting normally,' said Bernard. 'They were completely silent, and then someone screamed, and they all screamed together—"Whoo-woo-woo-woo!"' Standing separately from the local politicians was a group of men under a red sun umbrella. One of them had a red headband, and seemed to be speaking into a microphone. This was the *panglima*. 'I have seen politicians speaking to election rallies,' said Bernard, 'and they are nothing compared to the *panglima*. These people would have done anything he said.'

The next pictures were of scorched houses in Pahauman containing skeletons, one perfect, the other just a curved backbone, like a huge white centipede. Then there was a decapitated corpse lying on the road in a pair of bright blue and red shorts. The corpse's balls bulged in the crutch of its shorts. In one of the shots, the dead man appeared to have a head, but this turned out to be his innards, which had been piled up on his chest where the heart had been torn out.

Next was a shot of a ditch by the side of the road where two heads lay side by side. They were reddish orange, as if badly sunburned, the colour of people returning from a beach holiday, and what features were visible had become stylized by decay. A pair of dark eye-sockets. A rubbery ear beneath a slimy sideburn. They looked like pumpkins prepared for Hallowe'en and left out in the garden for too long.

I asked Bernard if I could make copies of the photographs, but he was afraid. These prints had been developed quickly, before the authorities had got a grip on the situation, but by now there were spies in the photo labs, he said. A friend of his who had gone back for more copies had had his negatives confiscated, and been visited by the military. If I was going to use them, I would have to take the prints.

Bernard was a poor man, with a sick wife. It hurt his pride to ask for money, but he needed it desperately. In the end I paid him £500, and we shook hands on the deal. We were, I noticed, both grinning. In the car, I caught myself giggling, a strange cold kind of giggling, as I fingered the envelope of prints.

Budi and I drove home, and he told me about his wife and young children, and the anxiety of February when Pontianak was full of rumours of ethnic war and imminent Dayak attack.

His elderly mother lived on her own some distance from Budi's house. His wife's maid, a Dayak, had left the city and gone back to her village in the interior soon after the trouble started. There was a big Chinese population in Pontianak, more secure there, it seemed to me, than in Java, where Chinese shops and businesses were still burned down or stoned from time to time. But there was a casual, institutionalized discrimination that had kept Budi out of the state university (his academic record had been faultless, but he had failed to pay his bribe), and made it necessary for him to take on a Malay name. Budi's name was like the white shirt and black trousers that he wore every day, the long hours he worked, and the mathematical precision with which he recalled facts and events—an extra effort of adaptation that had to be made to keep up with the rest, to start from where the darker-skinned competition had found itself from the beginning.

We passed a poster which, although I couldn't read it, plainly warned of the dangers of AIDS: a giant octopus wrapped its tentacles around the globe, above the stylized illustration of a condom. There had been two cases of AIDS in Pontianak, Budi said, both of them prostitutes of whom there were fewer now than in the past. There used to be a big red-light area: 400 girls worked there. 'It was so cheap,' said Budi, rather to my surprise. 'Five dollars or less—four dollars. Four dollars—you imagine! But it was a low-class place. A lot of fights in there over the girls, because people were drunk. But now it's gone. There were a lot of Muslims, Madurese, in that area, and they burned the place down just last year.'

So business had moved to more upmarket venues including, it turned out, my hotel. There I would pay seventy-five dollars; at the cheaper Hotel Flamboyant, twenty-five. For some reason Budi's knowledge of these venues slightly disconcerted me. There was a pause.

'You must have had a lot of Asian girls, yeah?' said Budi.

I mumbled non-committally.

'You know what? Javanese girls are a lot more...romantic than Chinese girls. They know what we like, they're not awkward, they know how to make love. Chinese girls, they're shy, bashful. They don't know what to say.'

I offered the unconvincing theory that this had to do with the traditional roles offered to women by the respective cultures: Chinese sitting at home with their feet bound with bandages, Javanese dancing erotically in front of their sultans.

'You're right perhaps,' said Budi, 'but you know what? You can have your own opinion about the Madurese, but Madurese girls'— he exhaled in admiration—'you should try it. *They know fucking.* It's amazing. I never used to believe it—my friend told me about it, but I thought, "Women are women—it's all the same hole." But he was right. It's not so easy to get it here, especially at the moment, but in Jakarta there are places you can go, massage parlours. I never believed it myself. But it's true.'

I learned later that this is a common belief among Indonesians:

Madurese women, it is said, have mastered a technique of strengthening the muscles of their vaginas which they flex dramatically during intercourse. The secret is passed down from grandmothers and mothers and older sisters.

'It's like they're sucking you inside them,' said Budi, taking his eyes off the road. 'How do they do it? You're inside them, but they're sucking you.'

It was the durian season, and the villages were full of trucks and tables loaded with the smelly green pods. Even with the windows closed and the air-conditioning on, the stink penetrated the inside of the jeep. I had never eaten them before, and the long drives and conversations were punctuated by the recycled taste of my durian burps.

One night we were driving back late through a burned-out settlement on the outskirts of Salatiga when we saw a light by the side of the road. Budi slowed and stopped in front of an intact house, the only one within half a mile. Even I could work out the Indonesian words scratched with charcoal on to the walls: JAVANESE, WE ARE FROM JAVA, they read, NO MADURESE HERE. We got out and found a family sitting at a wooden table around a moth-embattled candle.

They were the poorest people I had seen in Borneo. The man was hollow-chested, wrinkled and sickly thin. He and his wife were not old, but they looked more like the grandparents than the mother and father of the children who sat on the ground in grubby T-shirts. Their house contained nothing but a few rags on the floor. They gave us tea and told us what had happened here, and didn't smile or giggle once. I wondered about the life they must have had back in Java, to have exchanged it for this.

Like plenty of people they had sensed the trouble coming and left the village for a few days. But they had not marked their original home with the slogans on the walls, and the Dayaks had assumed that anywhere left abandoned was Madurese. When the man returned, he found his house burned like all the others around it— the place they were living now had not originally been theirs.

All the Madurese who had stayed behind had been killed. Even their cows were killed, and there were 'hundreds' of heads on open display. Six of the family's neighbours were lying on the road, without heads or hearts, including a woman of eighty.

'How could you tell who they were, if they didn't have heads?' I asked.

'They were my neighbours,' the man said. 'I saw them every day.'

'Were you angry?'

'No,' he replied. 'I was scared.'

A few more children and friends arrived and joined us around the candle, all of them with the stunned look of the very poor. They all started talking, in their quiet voices, and Budi was having trouble keeping up.

'I saw four or five children. No heads of children, but the body without a head.'

'When the Dayaks killed people, they put the heads in the road, and then gathered them together in one place.'

'They carried them there in a sack—'

'—the house of the leader of the Dayaks.'

Then one of the daughters ran up to her father and whispered something in his ear. Everyone fell quiet, and the mother began rapping her palm on my notebook and frowning at me. I slipped it into my bag as the beam of a torch flickered on to the walls of the house. Two figures strode up from behind us.

The torch was pointed directly on to Budi's face and then on to mine. The two newcomers looked at each other and laughed, and I was able to make out their faces. They were young men with long black hair down to their shoulders. They wore shorts and baseball caps, but were bare-chested; on his left side, each had a scabbard containing a *mandau*. One carried a thin hunting rifle, the other a bamboo spear. They laughed again, and sat down beside us.

The one with the rifle sat on the margins with his cap pulled down over his face, but his friend was chatty and bantered with the girls as they brought him tea. He was asking questions which, for some reason, Budi was reluctant to translate for me. There was an explanation of who we were and where we had come from. I heard the words 'England' and 'tourist'. Finally I managed to break in.

'What are you doing out so late?'

'Hunting.'

'What are you hunting?'

'Animals.'

'Have you found any?'

'Not tonight.'

He had a handsome face and glittery eyes. He and his friend were Dayaks, he said, who tapped rubber in the jungle near here. He came from Menjalin; he knew Pastor Kristof. His family lived a mile or so down the road in Salatiga, a wife and seven children. He was very proud of his children and told us their exact ages, from fourteen to one year and four months. He liked the Chinese, he told Budi. His sister was married to a Chinese.

'What about Madurese?' I asked.

Budi chuckled anxiously as he translated the question, and there was more unconvincing giggling over the reply.

'He does not like Madurese people,' said Budi. 'He says that they are thieves, and if they are allowed to escape to Pontianak they will just become pickpockets there. All Madurese must leave Kalimantan.'

'Where are the Madurese who used to live around here?'

'Some of the bodies were taken away by the police, but around here there are still a lot of bodies. Nobody dares to take them out of the jungle.'

I said, 'I'm sorry if this is a rude question, but you must have killed a lot of Madurese.'

'He says that he never killed them himself.'

I asked if it was true that Dayaks were immune to bullets, and he laughed.

He chattered on, talking about his sister and his Chinese brother-in-law, who was a businessman. After half an hour, we were such good friends that he shook us by the hand, and even allowed me to pose alongside him in a photograph. (At the sight of the camera his friend receded deeper into the shadows, with his cap pulled further down over his eyes.)

Budi's hands were shaking when we got back into our car. Much of what had been said remained untranslated, but he confirmed what was obvious: that the two men were hunting for Madurese who might have somehow escaped and secretly returned to the site of their former homes. They had seen our car by the road, and been suspicious. 'That was why they were so surprised to see us,' said Budi. 'They said,

"We thought you were niggers."'

Budi asked them what they would have done if we had been niggers.

'We would have killed you,' they said. 'Dayaks don't like niggers. All the niggers must leave Kalimantan.'

'He said that he himself hadn't killed,' said Budi. 'But maybe he lied to us.'

I thought: he lied. They were killers. I have never seen war, but I imagine that a certain kind of war depends upon young men like these, and that you find them all over the world, and throughout history, in Bosnia, Rwanda, Cambodia, in every civil and ethnic war. Young men proud of their daughters and sisters who hunt other humans for pleasure. They were frightening, but there was nothing mysterious about them. We drove back fast towards the Equator, a little less afraid of Dayak magic, but altogether more afraid. □

AFTER THE CRASH

INTERVIEWS BY RICHARD LLOYD PARRY
PICTURES BY STEVE SANDFORD

The interviews on the following pages took place at the end of March 1998, on the island of Java. In the middle of that month, amid Indonesia's worst economic turmoil for thirty years, President Suharto was unanimously re-elected for a seventh term by a gathering of 1,000 carefully chosen supporters. Over the next few weeks there were vociferous demonstrations in universities in half a dozen Javanese cities. Eastern Borneo, parched by a three-month drought, was burning with man-made forest fires. Faced with the collapse both of its currency and of international confidence, the government flailed, announcing bold economic reforms one day, and cancelling them the next morning.

To travel around Java at this time was to experience a little of what it might have felt like to be a foreign tourist after the collapse of the mark in Weimar Germany. One evening I checked into the best hotel in a small city in East Java. My room, furnished with antiques, opposite a palm-shadowed swimming pool, cost the equivalent of fifteen pounds sterling. Later, when I checked the latest exchange rate, I discovered that the rupiah had declined still further: I would actually be paying more like thirteen pounds. When I settled my bill, the rate had gone down again. The hotel was almost deserted.

At the traffic lights in Jakarta, the mobs of vendors who always pounce on stationary cars were swollen by the newly unemployed and by immigrants from the countryside. As well as the usual newspapers, cigarettes and souvenirs, they thrust forward a new article of merchandise: a glossy poster bearing portraits of Suharto's new cabinet. Among the new ministers was the president's daughter; one of Suharto's golf and fishing buddies had been awarded the trade and industry portfolio. I never saw anyone buy one of these posters.

The Republic of Indonesia has more than 200 million citizens; 120 million live on the island of Java alone. I talked to eight of them about how it feels to live through such times. In both Jakarta and the old Javanese capital, Yogyakarta, there was a sense that huge and transforming change was at hand. Many of the people I met were fearful; none had a clear idea what form this change might take.

Note: In the second half of March, the rupiah fluctuated by one-fifth. In what follows, 10,000 rupiah equals about one US dollar.

The guide

Haji Hadisukismo is a Javanese mystic, or 'paranormal', and lives in a village outside the old Javanese capital, Yogyakarta. During the 1960s he was an adviser to Indonesia's president, Sukarno, but left his service after his advice was ignored. He claims to be ninety-two, and attributes his longevity and his mystical power to the kris, or ceremonial dagger, passed on to him by his grandfather.

I would describe myself as a guide, as someone who gives advice. People like me don't meddle in politics, but we have a profound knowledge of what is going on in the world, and we are different from sorcerers and fortune-tellers because our inspiration is Allah himself. On certain days of the month, I hear a ringing noise from the three stones in front of my house. Then there is a sound like water filling my ears, then silence. Then the communication begins.

It's my job to be a kind of shepherd, and the two things that people ask me about most often are health and jobs. I advise people on their family lives, and can heal illnesses like cancer and diabetes. But these days what people want to know is whether they're going to be sacked. So many offices and factories are closing, and people come from all over the country, from Jakarta, Surabaya and Medan as well as from Yogyakarta. It's hard telling someone that they are going to lose their job, but at least when they know they can make plans for their family. If it's going to happen, it will happen and there's nothing I can do to stop it—I don't perform black magic. If you're a bad worker and lazy, you'll get the sack; if you're honest you'll stay. Well, it's simple.

Why is this happening to Indonesia now? There's no respect between husbands and wives. Children follow the example of their friends and don't listen to their parents. Chapels and mosques are in competition with one another. People move from place to place so much that they forget their ancestors. Everyone assumes that he is right and everyone else is wrong. There is a flood of know-alls, and no one is prepared to admit mistakes.

Even the earth is crying out, with these fires and this drought. The time will come when the power will pass from one ruler to the next. But the time isn't here yet, and we will only know when we are very close.

The talk-show host

Wimar Witoelar was the presenter of Perspektif, *a television talk show which was taken off the air in 1995 after it interviewed critics of the government. Since then he has begun presenting a new late-night programme, and founded a web site, a radio programme, a syndicated newspaper column, a publishing and merchandising business, a management consultancy and a public relations agency.*

Perspektif became very popular because it represented a certain something...nothing concrete, just an attitude of scepticism, irreverence maybe, alternative thought. It criticized the government by implication—I never named names. But the government started to get wary. I was called in and warned, and then I had Mochtar Lubis on, a journalist who's critical of every government. We made some cracks, and ten minutes after the show somebody called the station and said we must stop right now. The owner wouldn't reveal who that somebody was, but it was someone with power.

The new show is different, set in a café, with a broad range of guests, from very serious types—army generals and Ph.D.s—to Miss Indonesia, comedians and dancers. It's still going strong, because talk shows are cheap and there's an increase in interest as times get more critical. We are allowed to call in economists and talk about the financial crisis, and they tend to be from the opposition. Last night we were laughing about the ineptitude of the government, the clumsiness, the inconsistency. People love that.

Twenty years ago I spent a month in detention for anti-Suharto activities, and I don't want to repeat that. But it's so random, the political danger— it has almost nothing to do with what you do. It's to do with palace politics, the vested interests, and it's hard to follow day by day. So we just do our thing, and at least we win in the court of public opinion, as they say. I'm just a normal guy, but the country is uptight, so I look quite brave.

People criticize me and say I'm just talk with no action, and I say: that's right. I'm the talk guy, not the action guy. If enough people talked I'm sure there'd be enough people ready with the action. This is a new world. Suharto won't be thrown out by demonstrations, by 100,000 angry students. He'll be thrown out by fund managers in Hong Kong. And by talk shows, probably.

The demonstrator

Dr Karlina Leksono Supelli is Indonesia's first woman astronomer. She lectures in philosophy at the University of Indonesia. In February she was convicted for organizing an illegal demonstration against rising milk prices, and offered a choice: a fine of 2,000 rupiah (about fourteen pence) or seven days in jail.

It was in November and December that prices really began to rocket. I noticed it in two ways. I used to subscribe to scientific journals from Britain, but at the end of the year I realized that I could not afford them—the cost had quadrupled from 250,000 to one million rupiah. Even with photocopies you think twice—paper is more expensive and ink for computer printers has risen three or four times. Living costs for students are much, much higher, and their fees are going to be raised. But as the economic situation gets worse, the people affected by it most are women and children.

In villages, most mothers prefer to breastfeed, but in towns and cities it's different. The working environment is still unfriendly to women, and for mothers who work it's impossible to breastfeed. And then in February the price of infant milk formula went up more than four times—one kilo used to be 12,000 rupiah and now it's as much as 50,000. We thought hard about it for two weeks and then decided: yes!

It was a very peaceful demonstration, on the roundabout in front of the Hotel Indonesia. We sang 'Motherland', and prayed, and after a few minutes the police came. They kept asking, 'Who's responsible for this?' We told them that we all were, and gave them flowers. They accused us of holding an illegal parade, but the only parade was when the police led us across the road.

They arrested three of us and pushed us into an open truck, and we drove away with sirens blaring. Our trial was remarkable, the court was full of supporters, many nuns and many Muslims, all singing and holding hands. The judge was a woman. She tried hard to listen to our arguments, but she was part of the system.

If we lose our appeal then we will go to prison, because this is something that you cannot pay for with money; babies can't stop drinking milk and start drinking tea. When the judge found us guilty I thought: OK, this is a matter of justice.

The vegetable seller

Wagiyem is about ninety years old, and comes from a village near Solo in Central Java. For the last five years she has worked and slept on her stall, a platform of planks in the Induk Kramat Jati market in east Jakarta.

I was born in the Dutch time. I don't know exactly when I came to Jakarta, but I remember that the train still used coal and the ticket cost only a hundred rupiah. Jakarta was very quiet and very cheap compared to now, but you couldn't sell very much. It's much better now—in the Dutch time I couldn't buy clothes like this. The only cloth was the scratchy stuff you wove for yourself.

I grew up in a village, but if I went back now I could not work in the rice fields because I have no strength. In any case there is no rice. Here I can earn money, and it is safe—I have never had my things taken from me in this market. I have no husband and no child, but my nephew looks after me and my friend lives here. She sleeps here at night too, and she's another old woman like me.

If you ask me about the economy, I don't know what to answer, but it's certainly more difficult to get a profit these days. My beans cost me 1,500 rupiah a kilogram, and I sell them for about 2,000. So far today I sold three kilograms, which means I have 1,500 rupiah to myself. With the price rises, it means I can fill my stomach, but not much more.

During the turmoil between the Dutch and the Japanese there was a battle. I had a child, and my child died, and I had to escape. I had to escape again in the turmoil of 1965. I saw a lot of cows being killed. Cows and people. My husband died in that turmoil.

Now there is this new turmoil, but it is a money turmoil and so it is still better now. Back then we only had cassava and porridge to eat, and water from the ground. Now at least we have rice and boiled water. Before it was Queen Wilhelmina and Juliana of Holland, then it was Brother Sukarno and Father Suharto. It makes no difference. They're all just as good to me. I'm old, I'm a poor woman, and I can't tell them apart. I never went to the political meetings, I didn't even go to school. I don't have the words to say to you.

The speculator

Theo F. Toemion spent five years working in Europe for the Indonesian central bank, and in 1985 became a freelance currency trader; the following year he made twenty million dollars in six months. In 1997 he predicted the rupiah's collapse. He works at home in Jakarta as a currency analyst and speculator.

For a year, right up until last June, you'd hear people saying that the rupiah was 'robust'. In July 1996, there were riots in Jakarta, but in three days the rupiah recovered. The president was sick—just three days, and the rupiah was up again. They loved the rupe so much, and when it collapsed everyone became very scared. What happened, what happened? The answer is: speculators.

I know that world very well. There are 2,500 fund managers in the world, and according to the World Bank they have 130 billion dollars. They can leverage that ten times: that's 1,300 billion dollars. I remember '92, when the UK was kicked out of the Exchange Rate Mechanism. Even the Bank of England couldn't beat the speculators. Indonesia had about twenty billion in reserves. Intervention? Forget it.

Well, I can speculate, too. From '95 to '97 the dollar jumped fifty per cent against the yen, and I started saying that all Asian nations, especially Indonesia, were facing a readjustment. I called my friends, I said, 'Come on, let's play!' We bought the dollar against the rupiah. I predicted that the rupiah would collapse. I wrote it in the paper. Nobody took any notice.

Compared to Europe, this is a culture where people help each other and even though people talk of crisis, it is a crisis mainly for rich people. But I've gained a lot. I created a new business: companies need my analysis, how I see the rupiah going. With 500,000 dollars of my own money, I can borrow five million dollars, and I'm still trading. But I worry about the social unrest—it's happening already, although for the time being there is no leader.

I was in the car, the Mercedes, last year during the election campaign, and I got trapped in a big rally. A lot of people, kids on motorbikes. The traffic was moving very slowly, they were looking into my car, and they nearly jumped on top. It's dangerous for me, because I look a bit Chinese. I turned into a hotel. I was scared.

The herbalist

Nuni is about thirty-six years old and works in east Jakarta as a tukang jamu, *a vendor of traditional herbal tonics.*

Mixing herbs is all I can do, it's the only skill I have, and I suppose I enjoy it well enough. I was born in Solo, my family were peasants and until I came to Jakarta I was a peasant too. When I was thirteen my parents arranged my marriage. My sons live in Solo—the oldest is seventeen, and the little one has just started junior high school. I want them to be schoolteachers—even if schoolteachers don't earn much money, that's a respectable job they do. But I have to live here with my husband to earn the money to send them to school.

My husband sells noodles from a food cart, and I walk up and down here every morning and afternoon selling my drinks. They really work—I take them every day, and I've stayed strong and healthy. There are different mixtures, so this one is good for stomach problems, this one's for sportsmen who need energy, and this one is for sexual vigour. You mix the herbs with an egg, and with saffron or ginger water, wine, honey, and *beraskencur*, which is rice flour and galingale. The cost varies depending what's in it, from 300 rupiah to about 2,000 for the most expensive ingredients. I work from six until ten every morning, and then from two in the afternoon until five-thirty. I make maybe 30,000 rupiah a day, but in the area where I live everything has got so expensive recently. Before the crisis I bought rice for 1,000 rupiah a kilo or less—now it's at least 1,300 rupiah. Cooking oil was 3,000 for a litre and that's now 5,500, and so on and so on.

The ingredients have gone up, especially the eggs, but I've managed to keep prices down. My customers are nearly all regulars, all different kinds of people—traders in the market, taxi drivers, people who work in banks. The crisis is affecting them, but they take the drinks for their health and so far, with God's blessing, I haven't lost anyone. In fact, I think that in the last few weeks business has even got a little better. Perhaps in a time like this people need a release from their stress and their anxiety, and think that my drinks can calm down your mind as well as making your body strong.

The publisher

Aristides Katoppo is a journalist, environmentalist, and a founder and director of a publishing company.

I joined a newspaper when I left school, and every few years there were scrapes with the government. We ran an anti-corruption campaign and in 1973 the paper was closed down. I had to leave the country. I spent two years in the States, and when I came back I had no idea whether I would be arrested or not. It wasn't exactly that the writing was on the wall, but it was obviously too risky for me to continue as a journalist.

So that's why we started publishing—the dissemination of knowledge, but by another means. I suppose we're known for political books—biography, current affairs—but we are the Indonesian publisher of *Asterix*, that's our bread and butter. We really started feeling the pinch in the last quarter of last year, and from December to January the cost of printing increased massively. The price of ink and paper went up by three or four times. It's an irony that in Indonesia, a country full of trees, paper is imported—we have softwoods and hardwoods, but not the long fibres you need for paper, and local producers quote international prices. Indonesian publishers are shell-shocked.

In January this year, ninety per cent of them simply stopped. When people are worried about food, they don't have much income for books. And even if a book sells out, the profits it generates are not enough to pay for a reprint. The industry has come to a standstill. On the newspaper, the phones are programmed to cut out after five minutes—and these are the reporters' telephones! Indonesians are poor readers, and the reason is that a whole generation was raised in an atmosphere without books. That was the hope—that we were starting off a new generation used to books in hand. That's why *Asterix* is important—the children get used to reading and they take their parents with them into the bookshop. That's all threatened now. I used to order books over the Internet from America and even now it would be so easy—a little click, and it's done. But the cost has gone up four times. I visit the web site these days, and my finger trembles over the mouse.

The prostitute

Linda is a twenty-six-year-old banci, or male transvestite. He was born near Cirebon in west Java and works as a prostitute under an elevated highway in the Lawang Park area of south Jakarta.

Ever since I was a child I have had a woman's spirit, and I was the first *banci* in my village. But my parents don't mind and I go back to see my family three times a year. I have two elder brothers and three sisters who call me by my man's name, which is very, very secret. I've been living in Jakarta for five years, and three years ago I had my breast operation in Bandung. It cost three million rupiah, but I was very, very satisfied.

There must be 500 *banci* who work in this area. Most of us come here every evening at nine, and leave at about five in the morning, and sleep all day. The cost of play varies from 20,000 to 300,000—recently, we've had to become very flexible. If a customer takes me back to a hotel, I can earn 300,000 rupiah and that includes anything, any kind of activity, whatever the customer wants. But in the last month we've all felt the effect of the crisis.

Our customers are middle class and upper class, Indonesians and foreigners as well—Chinese, Japanese and some whites. But they're becoming fewer, and they all complain about the crisis and say they can't pay so much. A year ago I might have had seven customers in one night. Nowadays, it's three or four at most. There's a lot more bargaining these days, and the other *banci* get very jealous when someone else has got a client and they haven't. There's less to go round and we're becoming divided.

Food is more expensive, but I worry more about the clothes in the department stores. The cost has gone up—50,000 rupiah, 100,000! If I had my breast operation today in the same place, it would cost five million rupiah.

NORTHERN SOUL
Simon Armitage

Up North

I live on the border, between two states. I've lived here all my life, just about, and I know this place like the back of my hand. I know what I'm doing and I know what it's doing to me. And I know about belonging and which of the people are my lot—us. We're a mixed bunch, although it's all relative, and one of us is no more mixed and no less relative than the rest. Me. On the other hand, sometimes I'm somebody else, a face I recognize in a Yorkshire crowd. I'm you.

Bulletins arrive in various forms, telling you what you're like, who you are. In the morning it's the *Yorkshire Post,* in the evening it's the *Huddersfield Examiner.* At teatime on television, it's *Look North* with Mike McCarthy and the beautiful Sophie Raworth, or on 'the other side' it's *Calendar,* once the hot seat of Richard Whiteley, the I Claudius of broadcasting. Most of the stories reported involve animals or murder, or ideally, both, and occasionally make the national press. A couple of weeks ago, the national *Six O'Clock News* reported that pipistrelle bats from Yorkshire have a different dialect from the same bats just over the border in Lancashire. Under the heading 'Batting For Yorkshire', a scientist explained that the bats not only have a separate vocabulary, but also 'talk' at different frequencies, making it impossible for the two groups to communicate and mix. The bottom line is that Yorkshire bats have deeper voices, and are less chatty. The scientist seemed to feel that this was some extraordinary discovery, but to anyone living around here, it made perfect sense. The first village across the border in Lancashire might only be five miles away, but in terms of dialect and language it might as well be in Cornwall. 'Look', in their part of the world, rhymes with 'fluke' or 'spook'. So does 'book'. So does 'cook'. 'Look in the book to see how to cook' becomes a very strange business. If the War of the Roses ever kicks off again, this will be the front line, and anyone crossing the divide will have to keep their trap tightly shut.

You live on the border. It's a cultural fault-line, this side of it being the Colne Valley, West Yorkshire, the last set of villages strung out along the trans-Pennine A62. Over the hill on the other side is Saddleworth, Lancashire. Saddleworth used to be in Yorkshire until the Government's Boundary Commission recognized the watershed as the new frontier. One day a sign appeared at the brow of the hill saying OLDHAM METROPOLITAN BOROUGH in luminous green letters. The day after that, the sign was obliterated with a shotgun wound, and a hand-painted board with the word SADDLEWORTH was planted in front of it, finished off with a huge white Yorkshire rose. The council took down the offending object but a couple of days later it was back, this time in metal, and the official sign torn up from the soil and left mangled on the hard shoulder. This switching of signs went on for months until the council gave up or couldn't be bothered. Today, both signs stand next to each other, making whatever lies beyond a kind of no man's land. All we know is that this side is Yorkshire, always was, and on the other side the buses are a different colour. People setting off into Saddleworth for the day talk about 'going over the top', as if they shouldn't necessarily be expected back.

Marsden is a village of a few thousand people. One of your friends had the name of the village and his birth date tattooed under his heart but didn't show his mother for two years—it's that combination of rough and smooth. You live here, your parents live here, and the last of your grandparents, and your sister and her family live just down the road in Slaithwaite. Somebody once asked your dad how long a person would have to live in Marsden before they were no longer 'comers-in'. Your dad looked him in the eye and said, 'Fifty years, and you'll be dead then.'

The Pennine Way comes through Marsden. People who've 'done' the Pennine Way remember Marsden as the place they can't quite remember somewhere near the beginning, or the place they had to get through before they got to the end. Marsdeners are known as Cuckoos. They once tried to trap the bird but, to bring a long and not very rewarding narrative to its conclusion, they fucked up. Dimwittedness was the main problem, followed by a poor knowledge of civil engineering techniques and ignorance of one of the cuckoo's most impressive attributes: the ability to fly. In the next village along the valley, Slaithwaiters are known as Moon Rakers, having tried to drag the reflection of the full moon out of the canal. Dimwittedness again played an important part in this legend, though people of that village claim that moon raking was a brilliant and spontaneous alibi which some Slaithwaiters gave to police when they were spotted retrieving contraband booze from an underwater hiding place. Slaithwaite, 'Slawitt', is one of the most mispronounced place names in the county, second only, probably, to Penistone.

At junior school you supported Huddersfield Town, 'Town'. You'd been taken to see them by a friend of your dad's, who called jackets 'windcheaters' and wore driving gloves in the car. Town had won the First Division Championship three times in a row sometime back in the Stone Age, so there was history, and therefore hope. But because they were crap, you were allowed another team, Leeds, which was where your mother went shopping if she needed an 'outfit', or where you ended up if you didn't get off the train in Town. It was all very simple, until secondary school, when kids from Saddleworth turned up on funny-coloured buses, speaking a strange language, wearing red scarves tied to their wrists and carrying red plastic holdalls with a silhouette of the devil on the side pocket.

You were thirteen when you first went to Old Trafford to see Manchester United. Being a Town fan, you'd never seen 50,000 people gathered together in one lump, and you'd certainly never seen European football. You'd never been to a floodlit match either, and the teams came on to the pitch like Subutteo men tipped out on a snooker table. This was in the days before supporting Manchester United became like supporting U2 or the Sony Corporation, in the days when you handed cash over the turnstile and walked on to the terrace.

You were in the Scoreboard End. Before the kick-off, a man behind you leaned over the barrier and spat a hot wet blob of bubble-gum into your hair. Your friend's dad told you to leave it alone, but you messed with it for ninety minutes, and when you got back, you had to have a bald patch hacked into the top of your head to get rid of the chuddie. At school next day, you got battered for saying where you'd been, and battered again for looking like a monk. United went out on the away-goals rule.

You went away to college in Portsmouth for three years at the time when the British Fleet was setting out for the South Atlantic, and got glassed in the head in a pub for being from up north and for looking like a sailor. When you came home at Christmas you got punched for going down south and for saying Malvinas instead of Falklands. If the stitches in the scalp were a kind of 'keep out', then the black eye was a kind of 'welcome home', and you got both messages loud and clear. A couple of months ago, the Vice-Chancellor of Portsmouth University (as it is now) wrote to you asking 'if you would be willing to accept the conferment of the Degree of Doctor of Letters in recognition of your outstanding contribution to the modern poetry movement'. In your dreams, you're congratulated by a professor with a parchment in one hand and a broken Pils bottle behind his back in the other.

You worked for the probation service in Manchester for six years, driving round estates looking at bruised children, writing reports on smack-heads who were shooting up in their groins, listening to the coppers in the cells under the courthouse singing, 'Police release me let me go.' You once rushed a baby to hospital with a suspected cigarette burn on his chest. The doctor examined the baby and said, 'Where?'

'There,' you said.

'Where?' asked the doctor.

'There,' you said, pointing at the bright red mark on the baby's skin.

'That's his nipple,' said the doctor. 'He's got another one on the other side just like it.'

Before you parted company with the probation service, you were working as the Bail Intervention Officer at Oldham Magistrates Court. Every day was different, every day was the same. Every morning at about seven o'clock, you turned up at the police station, and if you remembered the passwords and key-codes, made your way along a concrete tunnel, up a flight of stairs, and emerged in the holding cells under the courtroom. The desk sergeant, if he was in a good mood, gave you a list of the men and women arrested overnight, along with a few details of the offences. If he'd got out of bed on the wrong side, or hadn't been asked to do overtime at Old Trafford for the big match on Saturday, you sat there like a lemon until one of the other officers finished his coffee and threw a bunch of papers at you.

The holding area was a few desks and telephones, iron gates at either end of a long corridor, half a dozen cells to either side, and a glass interview room in the middle, known as the goldfish bowl. Usually, there were five or six men in each cell, in various stages of alertness, ranging from the comatose drunk to the manic junkie.

In the goldfish bowl, you ran through a standard list of questions as they called the bodies out of the cells, one at a time. For most of them, you were the first person they'd seen since being nabbed, and after a year or so you reckoned you could fit the character to the crime without asking.

Puke or blood down the front of his shirt, asking what time it was: Drunk and Disorderly.

Calm and quiet, saying nothing without speaking to a solicitor: Possession with Intent to Supply.

Asking you to phone up and tell her he was sorry: Actual Bodily Harm.

Seventeen, wedge haircut, trainers: Taking without Owner's Consent.

Track-marks up the arm, saying that she needs the kids taking to her mother's: Shoplifting.

Eyes on stalks, a muscle throbbing at the back of the jaw, reeling off improbabilities one after another: Illegal Possession of a Controlled Substance.

Alert, mindful, innocent: Indecent Assault.

Terrified, short of breath: Manslaughter.

Silent, heavy, sad: Murder.

Angry, flabbergasted, indignant: Guilty.

Bewildered, tearful, compliant: Guilty.

Stereotypes—a stupid game to play, but there was a satisfaction in getting it right and satisfaction in getting it wrong. In any event, it wasn't as if you were judging them by the distance between their eyes. The magistrates did that.

Driving back to West Yorkshire through the cutting every night was a way of shutting the door behind you, watching the Oldham Metropolitan Borough sign disappear in the rear-view mirror. Always work away from home. Don't bring dirt to your own doorstep. Always set off to the west in the morning and come back to the east at night—that way you keep the sun out of your eyes. Always live where the rivers run from left to right, like writing.

Your front door opens out on to some of the most empty and dangerous countryside in Britain. Hundreds of square miles of saturated earth and rotting peat, a kind of spongy version of the sea. When you were kids you walked across the moors looking for dead bodies, but found tractor tyres instead, or fridge-freezers, or crash helmets, miles from anything or anywhere. The only other thing to do was to break into the air shafts above the railway tunnel and drop stones on to the Liverpool train.

You live just to the left of where the upright of one great communication corridor slashes the crossbar of another: the North, where the M1 does its emergency stop and meets the M62, gouged into the moorland over the back of the hill and completely out of its element. At one point, the carriageways separate to pass each side of a farm, and at dusk a farmer brings his cows through a subway, into his central reservation, for milking. Thousands of tons of steel pass any given point every minute of the day, but when the winter brings the motorway to a frozen standstill, convoys are snuffed out by the snow in less than an hour, and vehicles are excavated weeks later like woolly mammoths out of the tundra. The M62, like a belt drawn tightly across the waistline of Britain, with the buckle somewhere near Leeds.

From the observation suite of Emley Moor Mast, not much short of 1,000 feet of fluted concrete with a hypodermic aerial on top, just south of Huddersfield, you can see both coasts. Or you could do, if you were allowed up it and the weather was clear, which you aren't, and, even if you were, it wouldn't be. From Castle Hill, the other local landmark, the next highest pieces of ground going east are the Ural mountains in Russia, and you can't see them either. You can see the middle distance though, and you call it the North. The North, where England tucks its shirt in its underpants. It's not all to do with Peter Snow's election map being mainly Tory blue at the bottom and completely Labour red at the top, though that comes into it. And it's more complicated than women wearing rollers in their hair, and aprons, scrubbing the front step and boil-washing their husbands' shirts, and their husbands pissing in the sink if the wife's on the toilet, and their daughters in snow-washed supermarket jeans and crop-tops eating baked beans straight from the can, and their arm-wrestling sons farting in the one-minute silence at Hillsborough and turning over the mobile Ultra-Burger hot-dog stand after a night on the sauce, although that comes into it as well. The North can also be Lancashire, which is really the North-West, and it can also be Northumberland, which is the North-East, and sometimes it's Humberside, which is the Netherlands, and it can be Cumbria, which is the Lake District, and therefore Scotland. But right here is the North, with its Gods and its Devils; where Jarvis Cocker meets Geoffrey Boycott, where Emily Brontë meets David Batty, where Ted Hughes meets Darren Gough, where David Hockney meets Peter Sutcliffe, where Brian Glover meets Henry Moore, and where Bernard Ingham meets Prince Naseem Hamed, or at least if there's any justice he does.

It's halfway to heaven, they reckon, here in the county of Yorkshire with more acres than letters in the Bible. And you, you live on the border.

News Just In

A man from Halifax has failed in his attempt to earn a place in *The Guinness Book of Records*. After spending almost a month living in a tree in his friend's garden, he came down to earth only to find that the world record was not twenty-six days, as he had been told, but twenty-six years. The record was set by a man in Indonesia, who climbed a palm tree in 1970, and still hasn't come down. Interviewed by the *Yorkshire Post*, Mr Chris Lee said, 'I feel a right prat.' The attempt was made in a 250-year-old sycamore at an altitude of forty feet. Mr Lee hoisted up food in a bucket, slept in a sleeping bag wedged between branches, and took with him a supply of books to read, including the *Yellow Pages*.

A Place to Call Home

Driving around looking for a house to buy, you stray over the top into Lancashire, and call in at a friend's farm in Strinesdale, to find that it's been the site of a tragedy. During last night's thunderstorms, forked lightning hit the paddock in front of the house, and the cow that was grazing there was killed. It lies in a big black heap by the gate, steaming in this morning's sun, at the end of a long muddy streak where Roy towed it back from the field with the JCB. The cow was in calf, and a bullock in the same field—last year's offspring—mopes and mooches at the top of the hill, refusing to come into the barn. Waiting for the knackers, Roy tells you that for some reason cows are more susceptible to lightning strikes than horses, which surprises you, not just because horses are taller and therefore a more obvious target, but because they wear metal shoes. You also wonder how much the statistics for this kind of thing have been skewed by foul play, remembering what a vet once told you. During his career he said he'd been called to umpteen farms where cows had been 'struck by lightning', only to find a diseased corpse at the end of a pair of tyre tracks, dumped beneath a burned tree with the smell of petrol still in the air. Cows killed by acts of God qualify for insurance money, and can also be sold to the abattoir for meatstuffs.

Not that foul play is a possibility in this case. Roy retired from a job in the city last year, and all the animals on the farm are pets really, with names and collars around their necks. You can see that he's genuinely upset and anxious about the dead cow, but at the same time there's a kind of excitement in his face, as if something truly agricultural has happened, making him a proper farmer for the first time, not just a retired businessman with a smallholding on the outskirts of Oldham. You drive back over the border, across the motorway bridge at Scammonden, thinking about Roy in the JCB, scooping the cow up and tipping its great stiffening mass into the knacker's van, watching it trundle down the lane.

The next house on the list is in Barkisland, a quiet wooded valley in Calderdale not far from the M62 and on the right side of the county boundary. The property is one-third of an old mill-owner's house, miles too big and miles too expensive, but the estate agent was adamant that you looked at it, and you park at the top of the drive and walk down through a walled garden, between two lines of monkey-puzzle trees. The couple who own it are in their mid-thirties with a two-year-old girl and another child on the way. 'We're moving nearer town,' says Morag, in a Scottish accent infiltrated by Yorkshire vowels. 'Jim gets called into work so much, it's silly not to be nearer.'

Visits to houses nearly always start with the vendors supplying this kind of information, giving a legitimate reason for leaving, rather than letting on about the poltergeist that refuses to budge despite exorcisms from the Bishop of Wakefield, or plans that were recently passed for the siting of a glue factory and tannery in the next field. Another experience common to house-hunters in Calderdale is to find that the property hosts an electricity pylon in the back garden, and that a 1,000 megavolt power line passes within spitting distance of the front bedroom. Rather than drive around the area looking for For Sale boards, buyers are better advised to follow the pylons and the cables. All the decent houses are directly beneath them.

At Valley Ford House there is no pylon, but there must be a power station nearby to supply all the various gadgets and gizmos in the place, beginning with the music system. Jim slides back the cover of a cabinet in the living room to reveal something like the instrument panel of the space shuttle, and talks you through the various knobs and dials, assuring you of the system's value and reminding you that they won't be taking it with them when they move. In every room, Morag reels off the thickness of the carpet and the depth of the alcoves. Then Jim steps in with a handset, points it at a flashing panel somewhere in the ceiling, and the sound of Luther Vandross on CD or Danny Baker on Radio 1 or Richard and Judy on daytime television rises and falls as he runs his thumb up and down the volume control. 'We thought the wardrobes were MFI, so we were going to chuck them,' says Morag in the bedroom, 'but it turned out they're Strachan, so we left them in, obviously.' She carries on into the en suite bathroom, pointing out the shower unit with the wooden seat, the heated towel rail, the oval jacuzzi and the low-flush toilet and bidet, until she reaches the window at the far end. 'And this is the window,' she says, then nods at Jim, who draws his handset from its holster, and Elton John ricochets between the hand-painted tiles and the full-length mirrors.

Downstairs, you're led into a drawing room with a red carpet, red walls and a red ceiling, which reminds you of the surgeon's room on HMS *Victory*, painted that colour to disguise the blood. 'We call it the red room. Jim, pull the shutters to show how dark it is.' Jim closes the wooden shutters on the two windows, and we stand there in the pitch black, with only the pulsing of a tiny red light in the sensor panel above us, like a distant star. In the kitchen, there's an ornate wood-burning stove, like a green postbox, in the fireplace. 'Does it draw?' you ask her.

'Excuse me?'

'Does it draw the smoke and keep the fire going?'

'Oh,' she says, 'actually we've never had it lit.'

In every room there's a mobile phone charging in a socket, and so many pieces of communication equipment—faxes, modems and answerphones—that you wonder why Jim has to go to work at all, let alone move closer to it. The finale of the tour takes place in a cupboard under the stairs, where Jim demonstrates a telephone exchange that could probably facilitate the Yorkshire Water complaints department, with lines to spare. At one moment, he turns to you and says, 'But the great beauty of this system is that you can block your guests from making international phone calls.' You picture your mum and dad, staying over one night, surreptitiously lifting the receiver at three in the morning, foiled in their efforts to get through to Montevideo or Karachi. You think of the plastic telephone/address book you once bought them with the sliding catch and the pop-up cover, wondering if it actually contains a single number for someone in another country.

House-hunting in Farnley Tyas, one of Huddersfield's most sought-after outlying villages, and probably most burgled. Sandra, going out to South Africa with her husband's job, shows you the fitted kitchen. 'This is the griddle, this is the hob, this is the fan-assisted oven—you should knock half an hour off your meat with that—and this is the turbo grill, for barbecue chicken. Have you tried barbecue chicken? It's very tasty.' The dining table is a slab of granite, part of the bedrock that the house must have been built around. Framed in the bathroom window, Emley Moor Mast, like the after-burn of a rocket disappearing into the clouds. In the children's bedroom, she's stuck luminous stars to the walls and ceiling in their correct celestial positions. 'When I'm stressed, I lie down in here, turn out the lights and pretend I'm outside.' She flops back on to the bed and laughs, kicks her legs in the air, with the Mr Moon and Mr Sun wall-lamps beaming at each side of her, under the constellation of Cygnus the Swan.

House-hunting in Luddendenfoot, or Clubbenden Foot, as it's known. You follow directions down an unmade road to the cottage, where there are already five or six cars parked alongside the garden fence. Inside, the estate agent's representative is showing a handful of prospective buyers around the house, but as soon as you step over the threshold you become one of half a dozen disinterested parties. Clothes are strewn on the floor of every room, knickers and socks are erupting from every drawer, boxes of batteries and videos are tipped out on to a table, washing-up festers in the sink, children's toys—most of them broken—are herded into corners, and spores of talcum powder are still filtering through the air. It looks and feels as if some unmentionable practice had been going on over a number of years, which came to an end this morning, just an hour or so before the police arrived and turned the place over. A woman in a blue dress comes out of a bedroom with a handkerchief over her mouth. People pass each other at the head of the stairs and grimace. Nobody dares look in the bathroom. Through the window, the 'rock pool' in the garden is a puddle of piss-coloured water on a sheet of tarpaulin, covering who knows what. Everywhere the smell of damp, like a dungeon.

You go outside for some fresh air, and see that the gable-end of the house is built into a bank, which then rises steeply above the roof. More than that, it's as if the house is retaining the hillside, shouldering the moor, shoring up the whole of the Pennines which are ready now to slump into the valley bottom, roll over like an animal on to its back, burying the abandoned cottage and all of the evidence.

House-hunting in Holmfirth. You're shown around a three-storey Victorian house by Mrs Micklethwaite, who finally leads you up to the attic to point out the two rooms in the roof space. She walks to the far wall, towards a tiny door with a wooden handle, saying, 'And this is just a cubby hole, really.' Inside the room, which is about six feet square and without a window, three sons and their father are huddled around a computer screen, playing a video game. The father, his eyes fixed on the screen, raises the back of his hand towards you, which you take to be the 'Hello' of a man who doesn't want to be disturbed. Thinking about it afterwards, you can see that it also meant 'silence', and 'halt', and 'goodbye'.

Simon Armitage

Quiz Night Down at the Club

Question master: What is a topee?
Contestant: A helmet.
Question master: No, it's a wig.
Contestant: You mean a toupee.
Question master: No, that's a wigwam.
Contestant: No, that's a tepee.
Question master: Same difference.

Where There's Muck

To the Lawrence Batley Theatre in Huddersfield to see *Hamlet*. Lawrence Batley is a local supermarket tycoon who also has one of the stands at the McAlpine Stadium, home of Huddersfield Town football club, named after him. It's troubling that a person can buy this kind of civic respectability rather than earn it or have it bestowed on him by the powers that be, although for all you know, Lawrence Batley might be the most wonderful man in the world. And it's probably his name that rankles more than anything else, or gives rise to certain suspicions you have about him. Lawrence Batley. It smacks of a northern upward mobility—that give-away Yorkshire surname, with Lawrence to preface it as a kind of disclaimer, or something to separate him from the rest of the tribe.

Another groundless prejudice you have against him comes from working in a supermarket when you were sixteen, unloading slippery cartons of butter and margarine from delivery wagons into a stinking cellar under the shop. The shoes you wore went rancid, and on the day you left, two of the warehouse staff put you in the bailing machine used for compressing cardboard boxes, and left it running till you screamed. You think of this experience as your contribution to the personal fortune of all northern supermarket tycoons, and always remember the huge, hydraulic vice closing in, James Bond-style, whenever you push through the turnstile at the football ground or pick up tickets from the theatre box office.

In fact, being trapped in a shrinking space is not unlike watching tonight's performance, except in this case the torture goes on for three hours and doesn't stop until every inch of life is squeezed out. The leading man, as the *Huddersfield Examiner* accurately points out next day, could never be Hamlet if he lived to be a million, and Gertrude is the woman from the Nescafé advert who looks like Helen Daniels out of *Neighbours*. She appears to have a wooden leg, or even a metal one. When she falls to the floor with a clank at the end of the play, the man behind me starts humming the Gold Blend theme tune.

You're with Noah and his parents, which is interesting, because Noah's first ever excursion into amateur dramatics ended in a similar way. In *Murder at Deam House*, he was shot in the back by a mystery assailant, and discovered in a pool of blood by the lady of the house who was woken by the sound of a gun. As she rolled him over and declared, 'He's dead,' the 150-strong audience in Marsden Parochial Hall squealed with laughter, unconvinced by his departure from this world into the next. Noah is also remembered for having forgotten the very first line in his short career as a thespian, which was 'Hello', and which should have been delivered from the wings.

Noah's parents enjoy *Hamlet*, which is a relief after the hell they went through last time they came up north. Noah had phoned up in the afternoon to say they were visiting and he didn't know what to do with them, so you suggested a film, and said you'd go with them for something to do. Noah looked through the listings to find something uncontroversial and inoffensive. There wasn't much on, apart from a film called *Paris Trout*, and even though he knew it wouldn't be about fly-fishing on the Left Bank, he thought it sounded pleasant enough and a good way of killing a couple of hours on a Saturday night.

The first danger sign came in the title sequence, when the name Dennis Hopper flashed across the screen, and you saw Noah, four seats away, bring his hand to his forehead. True to form, about an hour into the story and just when things were going fairly smoothly, Mr Hopper took it upon himself to sexually assault his wife with what looked like a Coca-Cola bottle. As a scene, it probably lasted about a minute, but as an experience it took something in excess of a century to come to an end. On any occasion it would have felt ugly, cheap, unnecessary, but in those very particular circumstances it was a nightmare. In the next seat, Noah's dad reached into his anorak for his pipe, and without lighting it began sucking furiously at the mouthpiece. In the seat next to him, Noah's mother wrapped and unwrapped a Nuttall's Mintoe several times, finally lifted it to her mouth but stopped short of her lips and popped it into the ashtray in front of her. In the seat next to her, Noah glared at the screen, like a hundred-metre runner in the blocks, his eyes fixed on the finishing line. When we all filed out of the back door of the cinema into Bradford's Little Germany, there was a long and very obvious silence, eventually broken by Noah's mother, who said, 'The wallpaper in that house…was just like some your Auntie Barbara used to have in her bathroom.' It was the perfect response. We walked back to the car, slowly, and a group of students overtook us, reviewing the film, sounding off knowledgeably about screen violence and product placement.

Lawrence Batley appears in the December issue of *Yorkshire Life*, but 'the eighty-five-year-old with an ego to match his fortune' will probably be disappointed not to have made it on to the front cover. In fact, it's not until page forty-six that Mr Batley features in an article entitled 'Entrepreneur Life', under the heading 20TH CENTURY VICTORIAN, explaining his lifelong motto, 'The best is good enough for me.' Asked about his motives for wanting his 'name above the door', he replies, 'It's a massive boost for my ego, and if I said it didn't matter, I would be a hypocrite.'

Personalized buildings make a change from car number plates, but of course he has one of those as well. He stands in front of his big swanky car, LB1, a tiny man in a golf shirt and matching socks. The top button of his fly might be undone. He rests his hand on the bonnet and his knee against the bumper. It's meant to be a demonstration of ownership and pride, but it looks like he forgot to put the handbrake on.

The magazine also goes 'Behind the Scenes at Harvey Nicks'. When the Knightsbridge store opened its new branch in Leeds, *Look North* went along to report, with the beautiful Sophie Raworth coming live from the menswear section inside the crowded shop. On a large tangerine settee, a man from the firm's management with wide lapels and what your father always refers to as 'correspondent shoes', talked effortlessly about the demand for classic styles and designer goods in the prosperous North. The camera then swung to the person

subscribe . . .

GRANTA

SAVE UP TO 30%

© PHOTONICA

...and get a **serious** discount.

Subscribe to Granta and you will **save at least £7** and **up to £28** on the bookshop price—and get Granta delivered to your home. See the prices on the order form below. You will get four fat issues a year of the most compelling new fiction, memoir, reportage, argument and photography that Granta can commission, inspire or find.

So why not treat yourself now? (Or treat a friend? A subscription to Granta makes a great gift.)

GRANTA

'**Essential.**' Observer
'**Indispensable.**' Glasgow Herald
'**Remarkable.**' Scotland on Sunday
'**Wonderful.**' The Times

Your details

Name _____

Address _____

_____

_____ Postcode _____

O I'd like to subscribe for myself, for:
  O 1 year (4 issues) at £24.95 (22% off)
  O 2 years (8 issues) at £46.50 (27% off)
  O 3 years (12 issues) at £67.00 (30% off)
  starting with issue number _____

Details for a gift subscription

O I'd like to give a subscription to the person below, starting with issue number _____ for:
  O 1 year O 2 years O 3 years.
  (My name and address are on the left.)

Name _____

Address _____

_____

_____ Postcode _____

TOTAL* £ _____ by O sterling cheque (to 'Granta') O Visa, Mastercard/Access, AmEx

card no / __/ __/ __/ __/ __/ __/ __/ __/ __/ __/ __/ __/ __/ __/ __/ __/ expires / __/ __/ __/ __/

98F5S62B

signature _____

*Postage. The prices above include UK postage. Please add £8 per year for the rest of Europe; £15 per year for overseas.

O Please tick here if you would prefer not to receive occasional promotional literature from other compatible organizations.

Return (free if in the UK) to: Granta, Freepost, 2/3 Hanover Yard, Noel Rd, London N1 8BE, UK. Or phone/fax your order:
UK: FreeCall 0500 004 033 (phone & fax)
Outside the UK: Tel 44 171 704 0470
                     Fax 44 171 704 0474

sat next to him, a nervous-looking individual perched on the edge of the sofa, obviously not one of HN's regular customers. You.

Your mother, who's videoed the programme, turns up the volume with the remote. It isn't clear if the character in the picture has anything to do with the proceedings, or if he's just been dragged in off the street to say something. With a red face, he mumbles something about a clash of images, about fish and chips and Lady Di's smalls, and then it's back to the studio for a round-up of the day's other news.

'Is that it?' your mum asks.

'Yep,' you say.

'Did they pay you?'

'Nope,' you say.

Silence.

'Well,' she says, 'it was very good.'

Further North

With nothing much happening at the moment, and the bowling fixtures cancelled during the Huddersfield textile holidays, you drive up to North Yorkshire. You pull up in the car park in Helmsley, next to the enormous new toilet block built in the same style and stone as Sainsbury's supermarkets, and walk through the woods and fields to Rievaulx. In the Ionic temple on the terrace above the ancient abbey, a couple from Dewsbury are talking to the National Trust curator about bus timetables and concessional rates for pensioners.

'We can go anywhere we want now, for a pound, can't we Frank,' says the woman.

'I'm sure you can,' says the curator. 'Have you noticed this central fresco? It's been restored after one of the workmen put his foot through the ceiling.'

'Has it really. Because we'd never heard of this place till somebody told us, and we've come down today on the bus and it's only cost us a pound, hasn't it Frank?'

'Well, now you've found us, I hope you'll visit us again.'

'No, we shan't,' says the woman, 'because we've seen it now.'

Ten minutes later, Frank trips over a poodle tethered to a foot-scraper at the top of the steps, and arrives head first into the exhibition in the basement, followed closely by his wife, cursing all dogs and their owners. 'Come here,' she says, 'you've muckied your trousers.' She bends over him, inspecting the dirty mark on his knee and spitting into a handkerchief.

Directory Enquiries One

February. The telephone rings.
'Mr Armitage?'
'Yes.'
'It's Direct Line Insurance in Leeds. Is it right you're a poet?'
'Yes.'
'Are you well known?'
'How do you mean?'
'Are you famous?'
'Er...have you heard of me?'
'No.'
Silence. The sound of thinking.
'OK, thanks.'

The Tyre

Lo, all our pomp of yesterday,
Is one with Nineveh and Tyre. Kipling, 'Recessional'

You've just finished writing a poem about a tyre. In the first half of the poem, you remember finding a tractor tyre on the moor behind your parents' house, then rolling it down into the village with four or five friends, to burn on Bonfire Night. In the last year or so, you've begun to think of your upbringing as supernatural in some way, a notion based mainly on experiences like this one with the tyre, experiences involving some exploration or expedition, and quite often ending in mystery or alchemy. In a similar incident, you and your friends made lead ingots by melting down metal stripped from rooftops and windows, having discovered all the necessary tackle buried in the earth under the mill. Who'd left it there?

It wasn't unusual to go wandering off over the hills, just as it wasn't unusual to find things in the middle of nowhere without any reasonable explanation. A bag of golf balls on one occasion, a pram, the bottom half of a turquoise bikini, and so on.

In the case of the tyre, we must have tripped right over it, because it was sewn to the earth with tuft-grass and rushes, and the stitching had to be unpicked before we could prise it out of the peat and lift it up.

Growing up plays tricks with the brain, especially where weights and measures are concerned, and if in the end the tyre was actually the spare wheel from a Morris Minor, then so be it. But at the time it was massive; thick-skinned, hardly manageable, a huge monster of a thing, staggering blind drunk across the moor as we rolled it, using the diagonal wedges of its tread as handles.

You're more or less certain that the past, as some poets have already said, is a writer's only reserve. Almost all poems are the products of memory and recollection, as if the process of writing were an effort to recombine with that semi-conscious, half-innocent state of childhood, as if all poems were statements of loss. It's the same lamenting over the past that leads to so much anthropomorphism in poetry, and the sampling of inanimate objects for their human impressions to return to that dreamlike country of 'before'. Having come too far to go back, we appeal to the super-conscious to win out over the everyday and the commonplace, to bring about some momentary flash of reconnection. Words are the conductors.

You're also thinking here about the way in which very small children don't distinguish between the natural and the unnatural: if a toy train chugged across the carpet under its own steam in front a child, the laws of the universe wouldn't suddenly come into question. Once you were babysitting for a neighbour, and their little boy wouldn't go to sleep; you could hear him fidgeting and grunting through the home-made intercom between the bedroom and downstairs. After a couple of hours, you flicked the switch on the tannoy and said, 'Go to sleep,' then flicked back in time to hear him saying to the loudspeaker, 'You shut up, Mr Box.' Most people interpret this as the inability to determine between fact and fiction, as we grown-ups understand it.

In the second part of the poem, you describe what happened when the tyre reached the road. The village is down in the bottom of a bowl in the landscape, with all roads descending into it at a steep angle. This particular road is steeper than most, and straighter, and there came a point at which the tyre gained an unstoppable and terrible momentum. However much we tried to slow it down or tried to wobble it to the ground with rugby tackles and kung-fu kicks, it didn't even flinch, and carried on picking up speed towards the junction with the main road across the Pennines. It crossed the A62 between two lorries, going at sixty miles an hour in opposite directions. You sometimes wonder if the two drivers ever jump from their sleep as three hundredweight of black rubber tyre passes in front of the windscreen.

After the junction, the tyre careered on into the centre of the village, and we lost sight of it as it followed the camber of the street and turned to the left by the graveyard. Out of breath, with our hearts in our mouths and our hands black with the evidence, we entered the world of houses and shops, expecting broken glass and buckled metal at least, or at worst, the swatted fly of an upturned pram, with its wheels spinning in mid air. But the tyre was nowhere. The giant vulcanized beast that we'd brought to life had completely vanished; no one knew a thing about it, and being thankful and exhausted and children, we simply accepted it as a fact, and got on with the next thing.

There's probably more going on for you in the poem than there is for anyone who reads it. Your dad once made his living buying and selling tyres, so for you, those circles of carved rubber are a kind of currency or coinage. We'd be driving along some out-of-the-way road in North Yorkshire going across to the coast or up to Scotland on holiday, when he'd spy a haystack from a couple of fields away, with a sheet of black plastic over the top and half a dozen tyres holding it down. Ten minutes later you'd be sharing the back of the van with four remoulds and a pair of cross-plys, usually with water sloshing around inside them, and giving off heat like bread from the oven. Usually he'd pay for them, but there wasn't always anybody around to agree a price, so the tyres would jostle for room for the rest of the journey under an old oilcloth, like stolen sheep.

The only other time you saw your father take something that didn't belong to him was again on holiday, in Scotland, when he stopped the van at the side of a plantation of young pines, and asked your mother how much Christmas trees were going for these days.

It was the middle of a very hot summer. We kept watch both ways while he pulled and wrestled with the little tree for what seemed like an hour, until the thing rocketed out of the earth and sent him spinning off into the woods. He came back covered in tiny cuts, with pine needles glued by sweat to his arms and face, and passed the mangled tree into the back of the van, still hung with a great clump of Scottish soil. When we were stopped for speeding in the Borders, you had to hold it down as if it were a kidnapped child, and back at home he planted it in the bottom garden, away from the road, well out of sight. Pine trees mustn't travel well, or the soil wasn't right, or the shock of being attacked by your dad had finished it off. Within two weeks it was nothing but a skeleton, naked and shivering, and the rosebay willowherbs blew little fluffy white kisses at it from across the fence. Come Christmas, and maybe to make up for the failure, your father came home with a tree that was so big it wouldn't come in through the door. Always someone to use the wrong tool if it was nearer than the right one, he went outside with a bread knife and came back with the bottom half of the tree, having thrown the top part into the river. That year we had the only flat-topped Christmas tree in Christendom.

During the time that your father was in the tyre trade, you hadn't realized how tight money must have been, until one week in the school holidays when you travelled around in the van with him. It was a bottle-green Ford Transit, with a double seat on the front passenger side, and something called a 'tickle box' in the middle of the cabin, next to the driver's seat. What you remember about the tickle box was that it made do as an extra seat in an emergency, and that it got very hot, especially for anyone wearing shorts who happened to brush against it with a bare leg. Its only use, as far as you could make out, was for keeping fish and chips warm on the way home. Vans don't have tickle boxes any more—you've noticed this every time you've hired one to move house—or if they do, they've put them in the engine with all the other hot bits.

We drove around West Yorkshire for four days: Queensbury, Brighouse, Wakefield, Elland, stopping at garages and farms and mills and depots, but on Thursday night we still hadn't bought or sold a single tyre. On Friday we went further afield, places you'd never heard of and didn't recognize, out of his patch, and during the afternoon he talked less and less, and turned the radio off, and leaned forward so he was almost driving with his chin on the steering wheel. Every time he stopped somewhere you'd wait in the van, watch him through the wing mirror talking to men in brown boiler-suits who were either shrugging their shoulders or shaking their heads. These silent conversations always ended with directions to another place we might try, or in a map drawn in the dust on the side of the van.

The light was going and he'd just about given up. We were driving back towards the motorway on the outskirts of Bradford when he suddenly swung round in the middle of the road and pulled up at the top of a dirt track running down to a dilapidated mill. He seemed to study the place for a couple of minutes, with the engine ticking over quietly, then he dropped the handbrake and went bumping down the track towards the building. The inevitable Alsatian came tearing out of a half-eaten kennel, and was yanked back by a length of heavy-duty chain. Dad got out of the van and disappeared into the mill through a rolled-up metal door, and you sat there for twenty minutes, wondering how long you should wait before going inside to look for him. Suddenly he came jogging back out with a different look on his face, and drove the van around the rear of the building, into a courtyard where a man was wheeling a huge tractor tyre out of a garage, followed by another, then another, then another, until there were eight of the things leaned against an old diesel tank. You hopped out and helped roll them up into the van, using two oily planks for a ramp. Before leaving, you watched him put his hand in his pocket, but the man waved him away, and half an hour later we were back at the garage in Huddersfield, with three filthy mechanics hauling the tyres out into the light, and your father doing business in the tatty little office with the blow-up Michelin Man beaming through the window. You don't know how much he got for them, but when we arrived home and he put the money in your mother's hand and folded her fingers across the wad of torn and dirty one-pound notes, she cried.

Maybe if he hadn't done the U-turn in the van and gone bouncing down that cinder track, there wouldn't have been any money in the house that weekend. Maybe when he put his hand in his pocket back at the mill, there was nothing in it. Whatever the truth, he'd come home with a fortune, and after the tears had stopped we sat down in the living room and started laughing hysterically at things that weren't even funny. It was the same day that a polecat had jumped out at your mother from behind the washer, so emotions were running pretty high.

Directory Enquiries Two

March. The telephone rings.

'Mr Armitage?'

'Yes.'

'It's Direct Line Insurance in Leeds.'

'Oh yes.'

'You're not a probation officer any more, are you?'

'I'm not.'

'You're a poet, aren't you?'

'I am.'

'I'm afraid there's an eighty-two pound loading for that.'

'How come?'

'Higher risk category.'

'Higher risk than a probation officer?'

'That's right.'

'How come?'

'Entertainment and leisure. The public—nutters and all that.'

'I see.'

'Sorry. Unless you want to explain to us what it is you do exactly, as a job?'

'You mean for money?'

'To earn a living.'

'Not really.'

'Fine. So will it be direct debit or shall we send you the bill?'

☐

STORY OF A HEEL
Todd McEwen

'It stokes his lust but chills his heart.'
Catullus LXXII

My stunningly crummy apartment—there were big holes in the walls and I lay awake nights worrying about how they got there. It touched me when Jackie went out to a Japanese shop, over on Broadway, and came back with some things I couldn't afford and wouldn't have bothered with: a bedspread, an orange ashtray (this was 1973), and one of those cheap *sake* bottles, in which I immediately put pipe-cleaners.

The crappiness of this place, filled with damp from the unsleeping samovar of my enormous snoring Russian landlord, turned us on. The one time I asked Jackie to leave her shoes on was in this room. Often I didn't find her shoes attractive, though they were all expensive, but I must say the thought of having her in my lap NOW in her I. Miller sandals...

She appeared at my place late one Saturday morning, dressed for a party to which I hadn't been invited. She had on a pair of high sling-back pumps in forest green. They were peep-toed. Toes squeezed together are not so great. Because they remind you, don't they, of the bulbous summer feet of your fundamentalist Aunt. But no matter. I couldn't bring myself simply to ask her to leave them on (she was running late) so of course I had to ask her to wear them *in order to see if they'll let me take you standing up*. The difference in our heights had always prevented this without my lifting her up and placing her back against the wall. She agreed happily and turned, bracing herself against the wall, spreading her legs, looking at me over her shoulder—Jackie delighted in teasing me—but we found this was not going to be a feasible angle. I made a conciliatory noise. She went to the bed and lay back, batted her eyelashes and gestured me down on to her with her little hand as she always did. *This is it*, I thought, *dressy shoes in bed*, but shortly after we started she reached up over my back, undid the straps on her shoes and pulled them off. I was devastated but didn't say so—just the sight of her in the green shoes had given me quite a bit of enthusiasm and we, wow. She always liked to, on Saturday morning, before going away from me into the world of pretty uninteresting people at CBS, where I wasn't going to follow her, and whence she was already looking back at me, a callow and preposterously demanding boy.

Although one Saturday I did follow her, and in the flash studio, we—it's a place where they keep a camera warmed up for when the President gets shot. We were on a rolling stenographer's chair. After Jackie came she started acting like she was important around there. *We have different concerns*, she said, and ushered me out a scene-dock on to Twelfth Avenue. Well.

I attempted nothing with the shoes of Alice and Sophie—Alice was ten years older than I was and she had beautiful feet. When I walked up West End Avenue from her place it often occurred to me *I shoulda kissed them*, but I could never remember to do it. She wore thick-soled sandals of woven leather, which were sexy in their own way, though they didn't invite play. We spent hours in a fug of Jungle Gardenia perfume and an oil she put on her skin. We made a lot of noise in her neighbourhood near the Hudson, it seemed, for one night we realized this guy was eavesdropping on us from the street. I sneaked toward the window in the dark and shouted right into his ear and he ran away. This took my mind generally off Alice's toes, even though she did the nails with a pearl finish. Alice once screamed during what I thought was our least-charged encounter; it was so unexpected, given the lackadaisical nature of the event (we had become bored watching the tumble-dryer in the basement and reached out sluggishly for each other), that I assumed she was calling out in fantasy or boredom to her steady boyfriend, who she said was in Attica. I hoped it was true.

I can't remember why I desired Sophie. We'd shared some laughs doing plays. *Laughs*, what an expression. I found myself thinking I'd ask her to put on the surprising thigh-length black boots she had in her closet. Pirate boots—she might be Claudette Colbert as the pirate cigarette girl in a 1940s nightclub. I thought she'd look her best in those, on all fours on the shag rug (this was 1976 let's not forget) in her father's study, but it turned out she was allergic to the rug. Then she wrote me a letter from the beach talking about her *creativity in bed*, with who, bartenders. Sophie always wanted it quadruped, and if that is all you do, I maintain, the two of you will never make real contact and you will drift apart. Which we did.

But Mairi, O Mairi. When I am at my loneliest, as a man, I still regret the loss of her, although she was really rather peculiar. Mairi was honest with me about her desires from the start: she liked to be punished, wanted me to make up *reasons*, though she was a very responsible person and it was hard to find them—*you left the Rice Krispies open!*? So I told her I wanted her in high heels. She was so enthusiastic, she wanted to right away. The ones I wanted her in, black platform pumps with thin metal piping around the sole, with high, rather thick heels (please, this was 1977), were in a box of her junk up in Westchester. But the next thing, here she was walking into the room in a black tank suit and some strappy suede sandals that reminded you of your fundamentalist Aunt, and, to be frank, grossed me out. They were peep-toed. *I want to excite you*, she said in her most appealing Mairi voice, a voice which suggested ice-skating, beer and sandwiches, the naughty thief of her mother's cigarettes. The mere knowledge that her best shoes were only at the other end of the Harlem line was very exciting.

Summer nights, Columbus Avenue: street light and noise through Mairi's bamboo blind, marijuana smoke, wine and beer, Charlie perfume and the Eagles (again, this was 1977). Mairi would lie across her footstool, bottom in the air, her wrists tied as she'd asked me with her own stockings. She would stare, glassy-eyed, while I read, at her request, descriptions of sex from Mario Puzo, which were ham-fisted enough to match the Eagles and the unforgiving pot. On a cue I was to go into the bedroom, catch her leaving the Rice Krispies open, scold her, spank her and then we, whew.

What a lively marriage that would have been, that she urged me toward, though she wouldn't have been faithful to me. Mairi wrote hundreds of diaries, tirades really, in steno notebooks; she always abbreviated the word *important* as *impt*. The most impt thing about Mairi was that in New Year's week she went with at least three other fellows. I found the pubic hair of one on my razor—and then at his instigation she permed her hair, which I loathed. As I grew the more furious over her infidelities, she became contrite, Midwestern, retreating from her black underwear to nightgowns of flannel. Then she moved uptown, to the apartment of one of these guys! *To save money*, she said! I thought, *as soon as she sets foot off this block I won't see her again*. I was glad she was getting out of our neighbourhood. I became indignant about it in A PUBLIC SPIRITED WAY.

Todd McEwen

I consoled myself with dear Henrietta, to whom I've returned more than once, though still never at the right time. I 'loved' Henrietta so (you will see what my quotation marks mean, and a sad thing it is), she was so pretty and charming, that I never wanted to put my gaudier, tinsel desires on her. I managed to flip her over one night in a way that surprised her—you always have to be surprising her, that's her idea of 'life'. Whenever I rang her up, she said *You going to flip me tonight?* Once, after a rattling good time, very hard on a staircase in Long Island, she in a blue-and-white kimono, I carried this image of her around with me and wrote to her saying that I wished to repeat it, but with her in white pumps. *Like a sexy photograph*, I said, but that was more a way of talking exotically to her in a letter than a real request that she wear them. Although.

I told Henrietta a little about Mairi, and she seemed to react with distaste, but then during a walk through Little Odessa, Henrietta blurted out that she wanted a pair of *nipple clamps*. I looked up and down the street, wondering what Russian hardware store had given her this idea. And what about her statement when we'd barely met that she 'liked to be dominated'? More naive at the time, I'd taken this to mean in a kind of Desmond Morris sense and just mumbled, *hmm*, but it turned out some French guy (I *beg* you—this was 1978) had come up to her apartment in the Village and told her exactly what to do, *un, deux, trois, boum*, zipped up his trousers and walked out the door. She never forgot him. It. Most of the time my 'love' kept me wanting *equality* with Henrietta; I didn't want to think of her in these ways. It was because she had the most beautiful eyebrows and the most perfect spectacles, which she DANGLED, and because she smiled at me so warmly. Most women don't smile at me warmly—you can see they're just grinning and bearing it. I saw Henrietta last winter. We drank and smoked late into the night. It was snowing outside. While she was in the shower I investigated her dancing pumps and decided, based upon their colours and ankle straps, that I could do some restraining of her if she required it. I cackled like a Frenchman. *Heau heau.* But all we did was to kiss, and run our hands over each other in flannel pyjamas. We're *friends*.

Ileft the city and went north, out of pique, and found myself, thanks
to one of those hideous weekly newspapers, sharing an apartment
in Boston with Helene. Her mother and the Harvard Business
School had made her neurotic. She couldn't get dates, and didn't
know if she wanted to go out with men or women. Once after staying
the weekend at a festival of lesbian jazz, she rushed home Monday
morning, blew into the house in a frenzy, and phoned up this chap
she'd dated once or twice. He used to call up for her without saying
anything to me, even though we'd met, asking in an odd panting
voice for *Mistress Helene*. He came over from Harvard in half an
hour, looking rushed. Before he knew it she had her head in his lap
in the kitchen, and then dragged him into her room. She tied him to
the bed, put on her sharpest shoes, and for the rest of the day she
hit him with the belt of her Harvard Business School suit, and called
him names like *capitalist wormcake*. He was much nicer to me after
that. His name is not important. It was George Hackett. But here—
on a Friday night when neither of us had a date, Helene and I smoked
her sinsemilla and talked about sex. I would play my banjo and she
would put on her Harvard Business School shoes and give me her
mouth, a little, but the rule was that I had to, on her shoes. She said
wild things, watching me do that: *you and two big Samoans. My
mouth. Slicker by Yardley.*

So neither I, nor Amanda, had had any sex without a lot of
insanity attached to it for months. (I had been with, and not with,
Helene, and Amanda had been going out with a man whose name,
actually, was *Shark*.) It was snowing the night Amanda and I met.
She was wearing a pair of black boots with little spike heels. *Look
at the boots I bought today*, that was the first thing she said to me.
So we were going to do something, it was obvious. She had cherry-
red lips and used them prettily. She started to write me letters about
them, about her own lips. I travelled to Pennsylvania to see the lips
there. There was an afternoon on which a perfect women's-college-
in-autumn light was coming through her window. We would, very
pleasurably, for an hour (she was very good at it and would try
anything), and then she would work for an hour, naked at her desk
but for some family pearls she was keen on. She wouldn't let me talk
to her while she was working—I was supposed to lie in bed and

synopsize Ford Madox Ford for her, but while she was reading Milton I got her to, very slowly and rhythmically, which I guess didn't count. During a particularly rigorous passage late in the day I told her I'd like her in high heels—she was on top of me in her necklace. *Look in the closet*, she said, *and if you don't like those I'll buy any kind of shoes you want me in*. To think of an offer like that now. Gosh. I jumped up and started rooting around in there right away. But even though Amanda had some very classy grown-up pumps, down below her sweet dark overcoats, that *weird boredom* must already have descended on me, because we never got around to it.

And with Mary Ann, the wild stuff never even came up. I suppose it was that honesty-nullifying proper 'love' of the sort I felt for Henrietta. It just didn't seem RIGHT to put five-inch red heels on a girl who had such rosy cheeks, who took me to apple orchards and contradances (Mary Ann always waited for me *outside* of *my* destinations, cigar stores and very dirty bars), who played waltzes and schottisches on the fiddle. Oh you could imagine something, maybe, a tableau off the Tabu perfume bottle, but that kiss ends there, don't you think? I often thought of our relationship as being like the famous glass flowers at the Peabody Museum. They symbolized something, some *love of the good*, but weren't much use. The general Cambridge atmosphere of flannel shirts and dulcimers I found anaphrodisiac, though curiously I did harbour dark desires for a well-known Central Square busker. I thought she'd look marvellous in a plaid skirt and Louise Brooks lipstick and I told her this very late one night in the Cantab Lounge. After that she started to play farther and farther away from our neighbourhood; she's probably in China now. I never said anything to Mary Ann—the strangest thing we ever did was: twice in a row on a sofa. She said, *what are you doing?* which might have been an invitation to filthy talk, but was actually an expression of alarm, I decided, because I'd bumped her bottom with my, I think she was afraid I was trying to put it there. I wasn't.

All these people got fed up of me and I of them. I went and got a job in London because London girls wear high heels more and it made me happy to walk through the streets. Our secretary wore grey court pumps almost every day, which for some reason made me imagine her at the wheel of a sports car, though she came to work on the bus. She allowed me to admire her ankles when she applied her lipstick, hourly; it was an efficient, post-colonial organization.

Some pervert who made 'special' high heels in Hammersmith used to advertise in the *Sunday Times*. I took the underground there one day and walked past his shop, but the window was painted out and I didn't have the nerve to go in, *hadn't the courage of my perversions*, as our secretary said. I'd suddenly thought it might be the actual door to Hell.

Chrissie—was trouble. Trouble of the worst kind, that invites you homeward. I was suffering from the illusion that I was successful, that I could travel between nations, get things DONE. As a matter of fact, Chrissie began to suffer from this delusion too—she projected an equally screwy set of desires on to me: we'd marry and divide our time between Hampstead and Burbank, have cars, babies and so on. She would act and I would *churn out*—the phrase was hers—well-thought-of poems. Sure—*that's* a way to make a living. Of course I eventually had to reject this. But we had a London romance: we kissed on the tube after strolling along the Embankment. She was wearing some black lace-up ankle boots which, please ladies, promised things that she wouldn't exactly deliver. But she looked so sweet in them on that pretty autumn day. We had a long taxi ride out to Crouch End, where she was house-sitting. It was one of those nights when you know you're going to, you're both aching—her eyes are liquid and her every gesture is just short of reaching out, a stroking of things, you're halfway there and she can see it—yet you stall, you wait for the entry in conversation. (Chrissie once referred to me in company as *a very leaky man*, which I thought very funny.) Finally she said, ostensibly making up a bed for me on the sofa, *do you have everything that you need?* Just about, I said, and pulled her to me. We went to the beautiful, just-the-right-height bed of he who was being house-sat. I suddenly told her I was determined, actually, not to, it was our first date, I had nothing. But the cosiness of the room and the day we'd spent and her ankle boots led me ultimately to pitch her up on top of me. *God*, she said, looking a little pained, *what made you change your mind?* Just you, I said.

A month later she got a part in a sitcom in California and I followed. Our *international lifestyle*. She picked me up at the airport and we went briefly to her place before she had to get to an 'appearance'. She had on a Western dress, my li'l Texas strawberry blonde, and a pair of delicate cowboy boots. On her bed at three in the afternoon, as the car from the network honked for her outside, she leaned over and with great pressure of her hand, Chrissie got me to, on her red boot. I put on another suit and we got into the limousine and went across Hollywood to NBC. I watched her being very funny on *The Tonight Show*, sat there in the air-conditioned audience sweltering in my stupid English clothes, watching her lips on the monitors.

A few months later, things came down to earth. There was no possible way that we could keep up our relationship—her *accountant* wrote to tell me this—neither of us had made even $7,000 that year. It made her nervous, he said, that I wrote her loopy fantasies involving Hallowe'en masks and long gloves (this was the Alberto Vargas period of my loneliness) but couldn't come up with a single idea about our *professional future*.

On my next visit we were in Westwood one humid afternoon for her shrink appointment. I spent the hour walking around in a state of nervous tension. When she came from the doctor, looking, as people always will, troubled-but-bravely-smiling-through, I burst out that *we were going to buy her some dynamite high heels* then and there. I'd seen them up the street. *They're red and five inches high!* I said. It was entirely the wrong time to say this and I, even I, should have known it. God, I always ask for sex right after people's shrink appointments. Perhaps as a way of negating the shrinks; *such a hostile thing to do*, a woman said to me once. Then they spend even longer gazing off into space and picking fights than they normally do after their sessions.

What this darling said was *let's save it*. And what this darling did that night, even though her shrink had terrified her, and her accountant was bugging her about me again, and despite NBC's putting everyone on her show on two-week notice, was this. We ate and quarrelled and made it up, quarrelled and quietened it with TV, made a midnight snack and smoked Camels and laughed. I went to have a shower and on returning found Chrissie in bed, the covers up to her chin. She called my name and briefly lifted the covers up: she was wearing the highest heels she had, about three inches, conservative, bone-coloured. Peep-toed, but no matter. *Darling*, I said. *They pinch*, she said. I was touched, moved really beyond any kind of desire. But she expected, at least three times—such was the pattern I'd been fool enough to establish following her appearance on *The Tonight Show*. I gently turned her over and just as I had geed myself up she suddenly kicked her shoes off and I was suddenly left alone, ALONE as it were without romance or glamour, *without the gestures of love*, in an uncomfortable bed in a noisy part of Los Angeles where we had no future. We, long and sweaty, out of individual selfish anger and disappointment in things consequential and not (I almost wrote *things little and large*). She took a shower and came back in a flannel nightie. I was mad at her accountant too. When I saw Chrissie last year, in one of the Irish bars across from NBC in New York, she said, *those shoes pinched my mind more than anything else*. In that case you should've kept 'em on, I growled, thinking how she'd left me for a realtor who thought her show was funnier than I did.

I went home to Britain, and Robin, when I learned of it. I liked Robin's hair, her accent, and her *prose*, a pretty dangerous reason to go to bed, but she had a big nose. I like big noses. She was making funny political films in the north of England. We wound up in bed after a drunken night in Newcastle. All nights are drunken in Newcastle. And that became the rule: I took the train to Newcastle every Friday afternoon and got stewed *à la* Patrick Hamilton, waiting for her in a skinhead bar next to the BBC. She always put on this sexy dress before leaving work, the way schoolgirls change into hip clothes at three o'clock.

Robin was a Communist through and through. They get demerits if they even *talk* about sex. But she had this dress, and an amazing pair of four-inch lizard pumps (imitation of course) which you also couldn't talk about. So the whole thing made us very nervous. We would sit in her cold kitchen and have tea, and then a drink. She'd draw me out and sit on it, just for a while, and then we

Todd McEwen

would take the whisky to a Chinese restaurant down the street, trying to look as inconspicuous as possible in case any members of the Party saw us. Which was unlikely since on Fridays everyone in Newcastle is pig blind drunk.

I spent the strangest weekend of my life with Robin at a rotted-out resort town in the north, before spring arrived. We got there late on a Friday—she'd come up from London and she wouldn't talk to me during most of the train ride out to the coast, even though the whole thing was her idea. The BBC was driving her mad. We spent the night in a neglected hotel run by slow-looking kids seemingly bent on revenging themselves upon the absent owner. We later found he was drunk in the basement. He was from Newcastle. Dinner was surrealistically awful: the fish soup was loaded with unexpected charges of flour; I asked for salmon advertised in a 'delicate almond-honey sauce' and got a fish-shaped piece of tile with a mouthful of granola and half a jar of supermarket honey thrown over it.

The next morning Robin spent away from me, smoking a lot of cigarettes on the beach. I was resentful; I gave her an *orgasm* last night, I thought, though of course you couldn't talk about it. I knew I was just her anti-BBC-static device. And writers have to be alone during many hours of the day, no matter their supposed involvements. It was cold and wet. Come lunchtime we went up to a pub in the town and laughed a little; *laughed*, what a way of saying we had decided to tolerate each other for a few hours. An old hand there told us the owner of our hotel was barking mad. Do you know what? We stayed another night in that hell-hole. After dinner Robin strode into our room ahead of me and leaned over the bed in her ideologically suspect dress, spread herself in the lizard pumps. *No foreplay*, she said (they're not allowed that either). After we, I was looking out the dormer window at the depressing little estuary. Robin was smoking cigarettes on the bed and seductively reading Engels in her lizard shoes. *They say high heels are the preoccupation of lonely men*, she said. *Yes*, I said, *perhaps when the proletariat is united, no one will give a rat's ass about them*. But those lizard pumps as she made circles with her ankles.

But all of this, all this *pleasure*, got to be a routine, in my marriage. At the centre of my love for my beautiful and often rainy wife, I felt a deep sense of happiness. Isla was happy to oblige my wishes because I was her husband. It was part of 'cleaving to me'. The word *husband* had a significant erotic charge for her; in bed she whispered *impregnate me*. But we had no plans to have children.

I was half out of my mind in that little Scottish town, what with the people who lived there and had never been anywhere else, wouldn't admit there WAS anywhere else, except perhaps Dundee, ignoring altogether the realities of Glasgow and Edinburgh; the lack of mobility (we lived on a farm without a car); the palpable lack of my best friend, across the ocean, and all that went with him. But there was such a thing as a good Saturday: we'd go into town and I'd buy Isla something, a dress, or perfume, or a jumper. She loved wool and collected artist-made sweaters. *Here's his greatest inadequacy*, I think they might say, *he's always there with the little gift, and little else. Certainly no wish to think of the future.* Did I have the ability to make one? We would kiss and separate for a while. I'd go for the things of men (the division of Scottish errands), to the ironmonger and the newsagent and to Rattray's, the most beautiful tobacco shop in the world. I had *visions* in Rattray's, of poems I could write, which flitted among the old stone and silver jars of mallory and rappee. Isla went from shop to little shop for things she put in the tasty dinners she made us. Colin Campbell the grocer? He used to watch her legs. I knew. Especially after I'd given her an anklet for her birthday.

About one o'clock I'd run into her—she'd kiss me and I'd whisper in her ear that I'd seen something at Marks and Spencer, or at the shoe shop, that I wanted for her. Without batting an eyelash at the looks we got, we'd buy her chain-store lingerie (I was already thinking of the graceful curve of her abdomen). Then we'd walk along to one of the shoe shops. I'd pick out a pair of high heels for her, in a colour appropriate to the lingerie, or inspired by what the girls were wearing on the street. She'd try them on for me there, in front of the small mirror on the floor. The salesgirl always smiled. Once when I'd just bought Isla a lurid, very high pair of spike heels in electric blue suede, we watched a teenage couple in the same shop.

Todd McEwen

She was smiling, shaking her head and blushing, and held a pair of black pumps in her hand. Peep-toed. To each his own. *This is what you want? These? Are you sure?* she asked. He was leaning in toward her, in supplication really, saying in the low voice of embarrassed love, *yeah, I told you. Look, I've got my money.*

With these gifts to ourselves we'd go along to Moir's, toward the end of lunch. If it was raining I was so much the happier—in the rain I'd picture the fire we'd make at home, after our bus ride through the hills. On cold days there was a peat fire in Moir's back room. The lunch special, fish and chips, or curry, a glass of beer for me, and Isla always had a bottle of Sweetheart stout. Perhaps she'd join me in a Laphroaig, then, warmed, we joined the bus for the country which stopped outside. It took half an hour to get home and I sometimes made Isla wet with my fingers, if we were in the back of the bus, steamy with the wifies and their shopping. Once we climbed down from the bus and started up our farm road and she pulled me into the wood and up a timber track: against a big tree in the late afternoon sun, our presents in their bags on the forest floor around us.

At home with the fire lit she would start dinner. She put on her new shoes while she cooked. I'd turn on the radio, to *Jazz Record Requests*, and watch her walking back and forth in the kitchen. The music, from America, and the day, busy and 'urban' for us as it involved buses and shops and bars, made me feel a little closer to the life and friends I'd left behind. I felt, in those moments, looking out at the green field and the sheep, that I had combined things successfully, that I was cosmopolitan. I'd worked in the morning, gone to town with my pretty wife, bought her adornments, drunk good spirits—and now listening to Art Blakey we were going to have a good starchy dinner and then play.

One Saturday evening Isla was washing pasta in the sink, in a new pair of high heels in wine-coloured calf, which was what the boisterous town girls were wearing that autumn, with ivory stockings, and I had to have her that way. Isla felt my eyes on her and slowly, in little sideways steps, parted her legs. I went into the kitchen and lifted her short grey skirt and began, like mad. She didn't say a word until she was near, when she turned and jumped up on the draining board of the metal sink and took me in the front way.

I kissed her. Suddenly we both shook and writhed convulsively. It turned out there was a short circuit in the kitchen and electricity was seeking an earth through the sink and taps. (I repaired this but for months kept hoping it would happen again.) I carried our food out to the table by the fire and opened a bottle of wine. She, in her lipstick, and new underwear, and shoes—I fed her. She asked me to pour wine in her. In front of the fire she stroked me with the tips of her new heels, offered me one part of her at a time to play with. We held each other, looked at us in the mirror and spoke, each to the other's image, saying exactly what we wanted, giving a thrill of cinema to what we saw there. We went to the bedroom and another mirror.

But sadly after my electric shock I became dissatisfied with the shoes our town afforded. Some days I stopped for coffee and buns at a café before taking the bus home, and there was often a young couple there I couldn't figure out—they were well-dressed but too young to have been given any of the necktie-wearing positions the town offered (assistant bank manager, assistant hotelier, assistant hire-car ass). They'd drink a pot of coffee and moon over each other while I tried to read the *Guardian*. That was the year the town girls were wearing burgundy heels with ivory stockings, and she was an attractive town girl with the Celtic colouring I had grown to admire, like Isla's, the palest skin, the blackest hair, the greenest eyes. She'd rub her foot up and down her fellow's leg and it was then I noticed she must have got her high heels from a 'specialist', maybe that pervert in Hammersmith. They were the same deep wine colour everyone else was wearing, but they were five inches high (we were lucky to get four inches in town), with a hard calf sole instead of black plastic. I was amazed; all I could think was, do you wear them for him in bed, obviously you do, where did you get them? *Of course!* I said aloud, slapping myself in the forehead, *the Sunday Times!*

Our town was small enough that it caused a social stir when I asked for the *Sunday Times* instead of the *Observer* several weeks running. Normally they only had one or two in case the Duke blundered in. You'd think I was asking for pornography. The ad finally appeared. We didn't have a lot of money but since our love life was so adorable and we didn't have television, I thought nothing of sending off a postal order for sixty-five pounds. This is perfect, I thought, this is what a telly licence costs, my actions are reasonable. The clerk in the sub-post office looked at the address and then at me. *For my wife*, I said. I said this rather a lot to middle-aged clerks at the time. Everyone wants to think you're a sicko. Hell, why *didn't* I just buy the stuff for myself? It would have been a lot easier.

A week later postie came to the door as we were getting ready for work. *Package for you*, he said cheerily. They park furtively in lay-bys, especially in the mornings, and open everything. I knew what it was of course and checked over the surface of the box for rubber stamps and labels of blame, INTERCOURSE FOOTWEAR. Well maybe he was genuinely cheery. It was Friday and I thought I would save these for Isla on Saturday night. I took the box into the living room and opened it. She came in on her way to the bedroom. *What's the wee stiffie for?* So I decided to surprise her, the old male mistake. She was within her impenetrable and sickening miasma created by her hairspray, cologne, cigarettes and nail polish. *Something for you,* I said. She reached in delight for the box but her face fell quickly; it was almost as if she had been expecting something like this. Did you really imagine, I thought, that such a large box would actually contain chocolate? She took them out and immediately put them on. They were too tight, even I could see that. So the inevitable. You'll have to send them *back*, you're not *supposed* to send them back, how much did they *cost*, you must be out of your *mind*, we don't even have a *television*...And so stomped off to work (wearing them!) leaving me alone in the house with cold toast. So I began to feel very bad. I began to feel that it was absolutely necessary that I somehow *earn* sixty-five pounds sterling and give it to Isla that night. I didn't have anything to sell so the only thing to do was play my banjo on the street.

The bus, the snow. Not exactly busking weather, I thought, wandering through the town and trying to think of other ways to make money. NEED MONEY. I began to feel very peculiar, as if my personality were disintegrating. I went to the library and thumbed through some books, thinking that people might have put money in them. But of course the librarians would have found it. They go through everything. The snow lightened; it would have to be the banjo. But I began to be afraid of arrest, of headlines, PERTHSHIRE

MAN IN CASH FOR STILETTOS ROW. There are rules. Rules in society. So I headed for the police, in order to get permission. As I walked I remembered reading that in a book about obsessions, you have to get *permission*.

The vestibule of the police station smelled like a hospital. I supposed there were often hysterical people there, puking and bleeding and smoking. *Now, sir. Is it all right to play the banjo for money. Where?* Outside. *Do you live about here, sir?* Yes. I do. The big policeman looked out the window. *Your fingers will be awfully cold the day, sir.* Yes, I know. Finally he said, *there's no law against it,* and went back to his reports of crimes. I had several glasses of beer in Moir's, a mistake—wherever I selected to play the banjo I would have to go back into Moir's to piss, which would entail buying more beer in order to gain entry to the toilet. Or whisky.

I set myself up in the wind in front of the memorial to William Wallace, but it wasn't comfortable playing there. I kept imagining there was a sign in my open banjo case which said ONLY NEEDS MONEY FOR SEX APPARATUS. A neon sign. And some of the old men were giving me nasty looks for playing a banjo in front of Wallace's crotch. I then tried in front of the Post Office, which was too busy. People going in and out of the Post Office are in bad moods. You and that music of yours in the doorway remind them of the futility of pockets and money. So that was no good and I went back to Moir's. I asked the barman if I could play for money there, by the fire in Moir's. But he said no, Mr Moir wouldn't like it, Mr Moir thinks of this as quite a classy place. At which we both laughed very loudly.

I walked down the street in the snow with the banjo. I felt totally miserable. I had ruined my marriage and my wife hated me. I got a little indignant then and decided the only place to play would be in front of a shoe shop. People are happy when they come out of them. And it would be as good as announcing my reason for playing there and needing the money. Me with a sign, appealing, mournful, I thought, next to the guy who has no leg or needs a kidney—though they weren't stupid enough to be begging in the snow.

My melodies were plaintive, if curiously rendered on my instrument. Telemann and Grieg and a little Mendelssohn, the 'Hebrides'. Snow music in front of Stead and Simpson, worrying about Isla. I watched the town girls walking by, coming and going out of the shop in their high heels, burgundy and black, with and without ankle straps and some in smoky grey winter stockings, laughing: *look at their mouths, that would be a shade for Isla.* They tottered by as I played and they gave me money. They teetered and posed and laughed and looked at me carefully—I must have looked hurt—and put plenty of money into my banjo case. The town girls took care of me. □

GRANTA

I CAN SEE
Edward Hoagland

'The blind eat many a fly,' says a fifteenth-century proverb—familiar as recently as fifty years ago, when I was small and blind people were still all over, tap-tapping with their white canes and saddled with dark glasses. The canes, if waved, could bring traffic to a halt, and their rhythmic tapping could part a stream of pedestrians and function for the blind person as a kind of radar besides. Power and pathos: dark glasses were an emblem of the saddest, sharpest handicap. Ostensibly making it harder to see, they signified instead that the person *couldn't* see, and probably had a face so wooden or so profoundly wounded by loneliness that he preferred to go incognito.

Common problems such as cataracts or glaucoma were not often reversible back then, whereas today you need to fly to Third World outposts to encounter blindness on such a scale. This phenomenon of adults who were helpless and pitiable, though in the prime of life, became one of the first moral puzzles children recognized. Old age they knew; jailbirds they knew about; real freaks they might also have some vague acquaintance with. But the blind were ordinary folk, innocent of any crime or grotesquerie, of no specific age, who lived in a crabby or long-suffering perpetual night. A mean individual that I was acquainted with snickered when he told me how when he was a boy he'd snuck into a blind man's house—having watched him leave for his weekly tap-tap trip to the grocery store—and shat into the sink where all his dishes were. And I could hear the desolate groan the blind man must have uttered, coming home, smelling the evidence of what had been done to him, and searching for where it was, while he fathomed his impossible position living alone, as the story spread among the children of the neighbourhood.

In the 1950s, when I reached my twenties, however, certain types of people began to adopt dark glasses as a form of chic. Jazz musicians could dramatize the underground, persecuted, joky character of their existence and telegraph the idea that even at night they already knew too much about what was going on to want to see any more. Better for the spirit to be self-absorbed, ironically bemused, optionally blind—a 'spade' so savvy that he wore shades. Yet highway troopers, too, wore smoked glasses to mask their emotions and look formidable. And many of the newsworthy intellectuals of the era, café-based existentialists on both sides of the Atlantic, likewise affected sunglasses as a means of demonstrating that a great deal of the passing parade was better left unseen. Impelled by the atrocities of two world wars and signature books like *Nausea* and *The Stranger*, they seemed to advocate disguising your identity to limit what you let yourself take in of a corrupt, demoralizing world in which the night was better than the day because of what it screened.

I didn't agree with this, and didn't wear dark glasses. Believing in nature and an overshadowing beneficence even in its offshoot, human nature, I wanted to gorge on every waking sight. I loved the city like the country—the hydrants that fountained during the summer like a splashing brook—and wanted to absorb the cruel along with the good. I knew that Americans had responded to the bloody ruination of the Civil War not in a fashion corresponding to Sartre or the Theatre of the Absurd, but by turning West once again to seek the balm of the wild. I saw this because my own solution to a sad spell was also to head outdoors and climb a spruce, find a pond, or hitch-hike West to find the frontiers that were left. In the city, my response was to seek the most crowded places—Coney Island, Union Square, the Lower East Side—on the same instinctive principle: that life in bulk is good. Embracing the fizz and seethe of a metropolis was safer then, as was hitch-hiking, but my feeling for crowds has never changed. Rubbing shoulders with thousands of people, my spirits surge much in the way that I grin at seeing a one-year-old, or will approach an elderly person, optimistic at the prospect of talking with them; a basic faith kicks in. It's automatic, not ideological. I believe life has meaning; I find diversity a comfort in the wilds and in the city—that there are more species than mine, more personalities than me. I believe in God as embodied in the earth and in metropolises. I believe that life is good.

So, night or day, in Alaska or Africa, Bombay, Rome, Istanbul, New York, I never wore dark glasses. I can remember dazzling long days out in a boat in alligator refuges in Georgia, bird sanctuaries in Texas or Louisiana, scouting with wildlife experts who had some protection for their eyes. But I wanted to see everything just as it really was, in the full spectrum of colours, as a bird or reptile would. In the desert I was the same, and in Greenwich Village, at Andy Warhol parties, I'd no more shade my eyes from the blitz of strobe lights than put in earplugs. I wrote for the purpose of being read in fifty years, and how could you describe a world whose colours you hadn't honestly seen?

But nature played a trick on me. I didn't know it, but sunlight kindles cataracts, and in my fifties I got them bad, along with bad retinas. At about the same juncture a bunch of my writer friends died before their time of lung cancer, emphysema, throat ailments, and the like—Edward Abbey, Donald Barthelme, Raymond Carver, Frederick Exley, Richard Yates, and several lesser-known good souls—at least partly because they had ascribed to the equally romantic notion that writers ought to smoke, drink, fuck, carouse and get pie-eyed (whereas I only thought they should fuck). Not all of this chemical imbibery stemmed from the Gallic-Kafka-Beckett idea that life was shitty. Nor was it simply macho, though the Hemingway–Mailer axis of behaviour was as influential as the Europeans' despair. The hard-living ethos had its best argument in the idea that the mind, like a pinball machine, may need a bit of slamming to light up. Smoking like a chimney, drinking like a fish, or using pot or stronger dope might rev the mind, dramatize the vertiginous character of life, and wipe out humdrum thoughts for a while.

I didn't disagree with the proposition of slamming one's sensibility around—that's why I walked across the Brooklyn Bridge at dawn sometimes and had driven or hitch-hiked across the country eight times. Strangers and the play of expressions across their faces, by the thousands in a single day—Hausa, Chinese, Irish, Navajo, Polish, Puerto Rican—these were what the city boiled down to for me, just as it was the scores of species in the woods that made the country rich as it is: blackburnian warblers and moccasin-flowers, oyster mushrooms and oakworm moths, bigtooth aspen, squirrel-corn and hop hornbeam. The city hasn't worn quite as well for me in forty years of loving it. I love it more at a distance now, but remind myself that from my twenties to mid-thirties I chose to spend the height of the spring and summer in the midst of New York as often as out in the country. Human nature, if cosmopolitan enough, with bodegas and storefront churches and *kielbasa* eateries and elderly people sitting in folding chairs on the sidewalk and numerous infants, was nature to me. I walked by the Hudson almost daily, when the past night's paroxysm of violence or vomit had abated and the commerce of the day lent the city its terrific thrum—not just the million people, but the million trucks. I had a Bella motor scooter that I'd ride the length and breadth of Manhattan, or I'd go to a Yankee game and walk all the way home from the Bronx to the East Village, 180 blocks, as the daylight darkened. Or nose along the classic portal side-streets—Elizabeth and Forsyth and Mott and Eldridge and Orchard—off Canal and Delancey, where people were still beginning new American lives. Or amble under the financial towers at Nassau, Whitehall, Pine and Wall Streets, with that wonderful lift the beige and creamy and graystone downtown and midtown buildings can sometimes give you at midday, when they're so full of sunlight and strivers that optimism is lent to anybody who strides through. High buildings, high hopes. This was a special place to be and its enhancing identity was catching.

Mute, because of my stutter, I'd wandered Boston's night neighbourhoods with hungry yearning throughout my college years, supposing that maybe just to stare at a single mysterious light in a lonely house with enough longing would cause the woman inside, whoever she was, to sense my presence and slip to the front door and signal me inside. In a sensible world, a just and passionate world, it shouldn't be necessary to be able to talk to find a lover. After all, bad guys tend to be the best talkers of all. But I wasn't bold, I was shy, and such adventures didn't happen to me. I was a walker, a witness, but didn't *close*. One time a waitress in a café near the old North Station, where the trains from Maine came in, left me an extra dessert, but I couldn't bring myself to use this as an entrée to better things. Instead I'd walk for five, six or a dozen miles, feasting my eyes on the lights of the oil refinery in Everett and the half-darkened State Street mini-skyscrapers, and the harbour, where the water glittered and seethed. During my years in the army, mostly stationed as a lab technician at a hospital in Pennsylvania, I hiked round Philadelphia. After my discharge in 1957, I lived in and explored the hills of San Francisco, the prettiest of cities. And afterwards, for two and a half years in the early 1960s, I walked extensively in Paris, London and Rome, Sicily and Greece. I became a wildlife writer— a hook-and-bullet man—and began to forsake the city for wilderness areas, in pursuit of ideas for books. I continued to live in New York, as Audubon, Frederic Remington, Albert Bierstadt and so many other artists who have made wild places their subject matter have done (you generally accomplish more in the city because of its inexorable thrum). But I did spend three or four months a year drinking from a spring, bathing in a pond, heating with wood and lighting with kerosene in northern Vermont, and this kept me reasonably honest when I went foraging for stories in the Far West and Deep South.

My eyes were important allies in these endeavours. And in my anti-modernist ebullience I was not, I think, a Pollyanna; I saw the South with a Yankee's acidulous eye and the North with Thoreauvian impatience. (In my teens I'd been more drawn to the Tolstoyan mode, but couldn't sustain such exalted idealism and the literary aspirations to go with it.) Acidulousness is not absurdism, however. Sunshine and drifting water under a shifting mosaic of leaves, with alligators in the bayou and otters in a creek alongside— I mean, what more do you need to believe? In my travels I was seeing so many alligators and otters (once an alligator eating an otter), and waterfowl in flocks of thousands, and whales, seals, walruses, moose, elk, caribou, then African lions and elephants, warthogs, horned toads, striped skunks, black and greenish porcupines, painted turtles, white-tailed deer, ruby-throated hummingbirds, black-throated cliff swallows, blue warblers, red newts, golden eagles, water buffaloes, desert dromedaries, and little swerving brown bats, how could I not believe? So many creatures in a matrix of ethology that when I was out-of-doors there was never a day I doubted life's divinity. In the city, I went to and loved Beckett's *Krapp's Last Tape*, *Waiting for Godot*, and Pinter's, Ionesco's, Genet's, and others' plays as brilliant—but didn't actually accept the premises of absurdism. To a naturalist, absurdism is ultimately absurd. It's a subway/sidewalk/basement philosophy, a starless-moonless-cloudless-night philosophy. But there are few real cloudless, starless, moonless nights, and people living in basements and subways for more than a few years have constructed an uncommon life for themselves. Absurdism was like a stopped clock, but time doesn't stop.

Even my sense of divinity was visual. I'd never bothered to learn many of the bird calls in my neck of the woods, and knew my friends by their faces, not their body language or the barometer of the voice. I played great music drawn from several centuries all day long, but didn't focus on it as a radiant expression of humanity's special genius—not as intently as I studied the visual drama of the clouds and sun, the Hudson rushing onward, the pointy firs, fuzzy tamaracks, sheeny willows, generous sweet-sapped maples, or a hawk in a basswood tree.

But as my sight dimmed from the incipient cataracts, I found driving difficult. I began placing sets of binoculars next to the windows I looked out of, or wearing them around my neck. I focused, too, on bookish pursuits, as if my time were short, but postponing thinking about what was wrong with me because I'd always lived for the sake of my work, and as if I might die before it was finished. Even in my twenties, each night I'd made sure that the day's accretion was legible enough for somebody else to decipher if I kicked off. I've always anticipated a 'disaster' (faith in nature implies that you accept death as natural and often proper), and have always had weak eyes. Nature did not expect us to live to be eighty-four, or even sixty-five. Nature did not expect us to *see* so much, either—the daily TV catalogue of scandals and calamities, far-flung tear-jerkers and outrages that you'd think some day would end. You'd think that when the massacres of ethnic cleansing are broadcast everywhere, or simpler accidental tragedies like school buses hit at railroad crossings, they simply would never happen again. People would see the horror on the screen worldwide, and *never* do it again.

The doctors I went to for my blindness weren't sure what was really wrong because the underlying culprit, beneath the cataracts, was that my retinas were in terrible shape—'pitted and bulging like a bald tyre about to burst', as one surgeon put it. He didn't want to operate; the ordinary cataract procedure would be more dangerous because of the pressure that it would engender on the back of the eye. Indeed, the first three doctors that I consulted declined, and they mistook the primary problem I was having with my vision. They thought it must be the retinas, not my clouded lenses, because they could see through my lenses to the back of my eyes so much more clearly than I could see out.

Meanwhile, as my eyes weakened, I began to see the truth of that fifteenth-century proverb, and found myself swallowing flies or other foreign matter that might be swimming in my soup or juice. I quit driving and gave my car away because bicyclists now looked like mailboxes posted beside the road, dogs like cardboard boxes, and pedestrians like poplar trees. I was afraid I wouldn't be able to see a child playing there at all. I was living in the country at the time and thus became a long-distance bus rider. By great good luck, the carrier that ran between Bennington, Vermont and Manhattan—Bonanza—happened to have been founded some forty years before by one of my ex-schoolmates. It was good luck because I'm a shy person and in my previous spates of riding buses for long distances, during my youth, I'd never been able to summon the courage to sit up front and strike up a comfortable conversation with the driver to hear his tales of the road. I'd looked out the window for hours instead, which was its own reward. But now I couldn't see much of anything, and I needed an opening to engage the driver's interest in this blindish codger who had difficulty talking because of a stutter.

The night was not unlike the day for me, because I couldn't see either the stars or birds, either a plane's lights or a fox ranging a roadside field, or even read with my two eyes at once, because I had to hold a book or magazine so near that I was not able to focus both of them upon the words. I'd close one and rest it for a while, while using the other. But my straits weren't desperate. I had a lifetime of preparation for this, in the sense of jiggering my finances into position for long-term survival and remodelling the furniture of my mind for life's later stages. Goodness knows, I hadn't wanted to be blind, but neither had I wanted to be young for ever, and some of the changes I was now undergoing were amusing in their way, or curious, and an adventure. When I reached the city on my trips, I couldn't read street signs or numbers, so had to rely on my memories of its geography and count the blocks I walked from each big two-way cross-street—42nd, 57th, 72nd, 79th, 86th or 96th, or 34th, 23rd, 14th—to find my way, stumbling on the kerbs and listening for the lights to change according to the traffic's sound or the lurch of the crowds. Often I took taxis, but even this was complicated because I needed to pretend that I could see the route that we were following in order not to be led round Robin Hood's barn, and also that I could read the meter, after we arrived. 'What's it say?' I'd casually ask, dropping my eyes to my wallet, as I chose a bill by its placement, then raise them again and gaze at the numerals I couldn't really make out, at the same time that the cabbie turned toward me and answered.

I couldn't recognize my friends, and when I did know who I was talking to I couldn't see if they were attentive or distracted, whether they had had a sleepless night and a saddening day, or were feeling effervescent and mischievous. And by the time I had leaned right next to somebody's face to distinguish a smile from a scowl, the play of conversation had usually moved on.

My father, when he was first operated on for cancer, was insistent, even a bit frantic, that nobody in his professional life should know exactly what he had. He was afraid that if word got out he might be written off; that other lawyers would cease to count him as a player or think of him as in the running—a colleague or an opponent of any consequence. Similarly, I felt that as a blind writer I need not be reckoned with. No more reviews, essays or jurying; no more books to come out. I could be politely dismissed, and the good-time Charlies among my friends would depart. With glasses on I was seeing at twenty feet what normal eyes, without eyeglasses, could pick out at 400.

The platinum light in the early morning, as a gentle rain fell, nearly broke my heart—the tiers of green, each subtle shade different, ash and cedar, spruce and apple, lilac and dogwood leaves—beauty I was losing. I walked through the timothy and orchard grass, the tangles of vetch, the fireweed stalks and raspberry canes, each registering as friends I might not see again, with what was left of my eyesight standing on tiptoe. Hearing a toad sing, I would visualize him, along with the chorus of tree frogs in the alder thicket, rejoicing in the rain. My dog I saw because he came to my hands, and birches became my favourite trees (except in July when the basswoods bloomed with that fetching, incomparable scent that was Thoreau's favourite also), because their white bark glowed.

I bought a telescope to gaze at the rising moon, sometimes

following its slow-scudding trajectory through much of an evening, and wore field glasses all day, ready to peer through a window if I heard a car turn into the driveway or if the wind blew and I wanted to see the crowns of the trees bob and interlace. But I was generally too late; by the time I located the car, it would be too close to stare at discreetly, and a bird—if I heard a bird sing—would have hopped to another branch or taken flight before I got it into focus. Still, just having these eight-power lenses to clap in front of my regular glasses was a comfort, though already I could feel they'd be no help if I went truly blind.

As the curtain drew tighter, closing my horizon from a hundred to sixty and then thirty feet, I saved my spirits from thoroughly sinking by paying attention to the peculiar details of what was happening to me and how to continue functioning. I hitch-hiked to my teaching job and home, thumb-up, like a boy again; I'd done so much of that in my teens. I mapped the seating of my classes, asking the students to sit in the same place each week so I would know who was speaking, and to speak without first raising their hands. Walking to town, I focused upon my lungs and legs, and itemized the feel of the weather, or the menu of colours my eyes still took in, after shadings became a blur. I listened to Dickens and Shakespeare on tape, and experimented with radio snacking.

There are fair-weather friends and foul-weather friends, and we need both kinds in our lives, especially so because each is likely to absent himself rather abruptly when the wind shifts. The drama of an emergency may unsettle a fair-weather specialist, uncorking alarming vibrations of vertigo in him, and cause him to make his excuses and discreetly flee. But the same intimations of pervasive catastrophe will give the foul-weather person a bracing sense that life is, indeed, dangerous and interesting. The proverbial social worker, who is an absolute ace at her work but only manages to hold her own hang-ups in check by focusing hard on her clients', is an example. But of course it is she who pulls people through their crises, not your sunnier, more politic soul who avoids the taint of misery. On the other hand, when you bask in good news and things are going fine, an ambulance-chaser may not be your best bet for a drinking buddy. He'll be listening for the crump of thunder, the winds of a cyclone just over the horizon, as if your good luck cannot last. You want summer soldiers then.

My summer soldiers were now cancelling lunch dates, quietly dropping me from party lists and tacitly waiting to see if my eye problems were going to sort themselves out, like other difficulties, financial, legal, personal, that sometimes throw a wrench into a person's career and remove him from circulation for a spell. We were at an age when people we knew were beginning to die off anyway and get dropped from everybody's address books. But unlike other things that plague us, blindness—to be alive yet denied the chief measure of enjoying life—is often studied in Sunday school as a kind of paradigm. Even as kids we could approximate the experience just by closing our eyes. You couldn't do that with cancer, or other unambiguous disasters. But why were people rendered blind, born blind—squeezed into inhabiting only their fingertips and ears? We could not answer this.

The ethic of pity was what we were taught to feel with regard to blind people. The taboo against bumping or cheating or tripping them up was extreme. So wicked a notion could scarcely provoke a titter, it was so terrible; and hearing that story of the boy we knew who'd snuck into the blind man's house and shat in his sink—it was so wild we couldn't believe it, then couldn't restrain our ugly giggles. To imagine his wail of despair and throttled horror, the disgust and dread the man must have felt when he returned, sniffed incredulously, searched and finally ran his hand against the turds, or maybe set his dishes down in them all unawares...this lay beyond the bounds of civilization. And the perpetrator remained unusual. The last time I saw him, he was in his fifties and said that he had bought a pair of binoculars to watch a lonesome spinster woman who lived across the road, who he said was 'going to hang herself for sure one day'. He was waiting for the morning when he would see her stringy body strung from a rafter—her misery having got the best of her.

One rarely hears of anybody suffering some variety of biblical self-loathing because of their past cruelty to others. Mostly they sit in church, vote, shop, and deal in goods or services like anybody else. They're anaesthetized, living well and in denial; and nothing wakes them up. But when I left home for a series of cheap hotels in New

York during my twenties, while I was setting my course as a writer, I used to know several blind men and women who'd been stranded in these bleak establishments by the social agencies and their own lack of money. Though generally innocents, they were living like 'sinners in the hands of an angry god', squirming upon a griddle of petty fears and pilferage, morning humiliations and afternoon griefs, while the genuine sinners in high-rises along Central Park West a few blocks away lived high off the hog. They'd grope along the walls in the endless shabby corridors or through the lobby, its floor tilting, to get out to the street to feel the sunshine on their faces and buy a can of tuna fish and a quart of orange juice.

Tuna is indeed a comfort, if you pay attention to it—tasting of the sea, in fact the very salts of life—and so is orange juice, which opulently personifies the sweet acidity of roots, sunshine and trees. When I was blind I loved to savour juices—grapefruit, apple cider and V-8—all of which, considering the pleasure they give, seemed unbelievably available and inexpensive. But the problem for these blind people was just procuring the food, or going to the common bathroom at the corner of the hall with a gauntlet of other souls eyeing them on the way with the vibrations of satisfaction that come from seeing someone worse off than you are. The women sometimes got manhandled in alcoves off the stairs, the lobby, or the elevator as they made their way down to the coffee shop, by old men who lay in wait along the route they had to follow, and 'copped a feel' under the pretext of assisting them over a set of steps or around a pail. Gracious, what despair they must have felt as the months and years ground on—the hopeless tar pit they had fallen into! No end to how precarious their daily position was—and just the jabbering talk-show hosts on the radio for company—except for one tragic and unlucky lady whom I'd known slightly, who was burned alive when the hotel that the Welfare Department had beached her in caught fire, and the various crummy sighted men who used to grope her in the corridors when she left her room forgot all about her until the place had become an inferno. They remembered on the sidewalk.

Blind, I could no longer go to museums (would have had to stand so close my glasses scratched the paintings). I couldn't see butterflies and realized that unlike the kingdom of birds these white admirals and tiger swallowtails were totally lost to me. At least I had tapes of bird calls, but this meant only that I was learning to recognize the calls of warblers and other little woods birds that I'd never bothered to track down and actually look at while I still had my sight.

Blindness, as one feels it from inside, is like a shutdown of the front wall of one's head. The ears—at both sides—are left, but one's eyes, useless now, seem to have constituted one's entire forehead and face, north of one's nose. And what wouldn't one sacrifice to get them back! I would have eaten out of garbage cans, gone friendless, given my possessions away or surrendered a leg to be able to see grass wave in the wind, not just hear it—see whose footsteps were approaching, not have to wait until people chose to speak. My regret was so comprehensive that I seldom spoke of it, just as, when you visit a dying person, only seldom do they blurt out, *Oh god, I'm disappointed! I'm losing everything I've loved and cared for, everything important to me!*

Instead I apologized as charmingly as I could when I reached for what I thought was my wine at somebody's dinner party and put my hand into the cranberry sauce, or tripped over a coffee table, spilling the pot and six people's cups. I improvised ways to disguise how sightless I was by keeping my face wisely turned toward whoever was speaking and recognizing my acquaintances by their morphs and stoops, their irascibility or depression, anxiety or kindness. I learned to listen urgently for the click of a stop-light on the street, and to assign my students only books that I had read intensively before, staving off the time when I would be too disabled to teach.

In H. G. Wells's short story, 'The Country of the Blind', a sighted wanderer enters a precipitous valley peopled entirely by the congenitally blind. At first he gloats, remembering the folk adage that 'In the country of the blind the one-eyed man is King.' But it turns out that they can trace and chase and capture him by their super-sense of sound, and after they do so, and have humoured him a bit, they decide to 'operate' on him for his own good to remove the 'growths' in his eye sockets that appear to them to be at the root of his abnormality. Though he's fallen in love with a young woman who often has mediated for him, she too wants him normalized. The jelly of his eyes, she realizes, is the source of what she regards as his hallucinations, and therefore of friction between them. Oddity can never reign; and so he flees to freeze in the snows above the valley, alone and in the ecstasy of eyesight, rather than submit to being blinded by them.

Quite so. I discovered that sight was an ecstasy next to which sex, for example, was small potatoes. Watching raindrops running down a window and the grey sky's purplish bellying and the trembling trees, I gorged on what I could still manage to see. I studied seed-heads through my telescope—and the scrimshaw on the moon—and a balm of Gilead's intricacy of boughs. Lying down next to a brook, I watched the amber water ripple, the yellow miracle of moss. I laid my head next to individual rocks, or underneath a pine whose million needles were a sunburst, and above them fishbone clouds. Black crows; the greenish-bluish tawny grasses; a red sweatshirt; or a white birch's beckoning bark. Nothing else—not speech or smell or hearing—matters like your eyes. In the city I would try frantically to find an address that I had to get to, but would be unable to read the numerals on the buildings or the streets, and stutter so badly that the people I asked for help dodged by me as they would a madman.

Walking had always been one of life's centrepieces for me, especially in the city, where it enabled me to pack in enough joy, sensation and exercise to make up for the deficits of living there. Seventy, eighty blocks hadn't seemed a lot, and when younger I had been a whirlwind walker, attentive to developments a hundred yards ahead (this, along with my native New Yorker street smarts, had kept me safe for decades). Good eyes had helped me finesse, too, the more pressing threat of having to speak. My boyhood stutter, which extended well past middle age, made me appear not simply importunate like a bum or beggar but disoriented and deranged—my mouth flabbering, my expression wounded, needy, fatalistic. Thus, for any information I needed, it was imperative that in the second or two I had before a respectable citizen brushed by me assuming I was homeless and a panhandler, I convince him I was handicapped, not one of the legion of beseechers inhabiting the street. And it was so searing to be rebuffed—I *did* feel homeless then—that until I had gone semi-blind, I would search and search to almost any lengths to avoid asking directions. But, blind, losing the confident posture and direct, lively eyes of somebody on top of life, I really did begin to look like an alcoholic pleading for a quarter, or flipping out. The experience of being mistaken for a derelict is only briefly beneficial to the soul; and as a stutterer for more than fifty years, I'd been scalded by such episodes often enough already.

My career as writer and teacher was stalling. I couldn't read my students' essays, and had to stop reviewing books. The travel assignments that I coveted dried up because when an editor took me out to lunch he would notice me bumping into hydrants. I thought of reinventing myself as an author of children's stories. Like poems, they'd be short enough to rewrite in my head and dictate later. Otter and muskrat, snake and frog, fox and woodchuck, owl and squirrel, cowbird and warbler, coyote and rabbit—these would be my characters. But, disheartened on the darkening streets where my thwarted haste was just a mote in New York's pariah population, I simply wept at times—my badge of misery so commonplace. In the country, friends shrunk farther into the haze, as if in a science fiction novel, though of course it was I who was shrinking. 'Good to see you,' I once said, in parting, whereupon the childhood doggerel echoed in my mind: *I see, said the blind man, but he didn't see at all.*

Then, curiously, my stutter began to lighten, as if it were at the far end of a seesaw from this infinitely more serious problem. Stuttering is probably hereditary, but in degree or severity it's also the servant of emotions such as self-consciousness, embarrassment, and other low-grade fears and agitations that tend to feed upon themselves. Yet my mind was thrown out of its accustomed tics and potholes. The downward spiral or vicious circle, which had worn deep ruts in my synapses over the course of half a century, was broken by the pitch of urgency of this much worse emergency. Adrenalin, too, always helpful, kicked in, and instead of getting depressed I could rise to a challenge with a kind of Battle-of-Britain exuberance, could quit stuttering, crack a joke and ask for assistance with straightforward good humour. As I saw less, I felt liberated to chat with strangers because I knew I wouldn't see their silent laughter if my difficulties aroused their *schadenfreude*. Though I hadn't had a chance to tunnel beneath the wreckage and find the detours that blind people use, such as a whetted sense of hearing or aggrandized fingers, curiosity pepped my spirits. It's what makes war fun—coping, camouflaging—and thus at parties I could often speak better under the stress of not being able to see. But if you can't make out the mood or identity of the person you are talking to, or discern who is across the room, and have to cadge a ride somehow in order to get home, the bravery of blindness remains only a small advantage.

Sex was another story. Touch and imagination, being equal legs of a tripod, can fill in splendidly for fading eyes. Sex became an intense focus for me. At fifty-seven, fifty-eight, I was making love as often as ten times a week, both for solace and to insist to my partner, *Don't count me out!* This eyelessly frenetic pace was a survival tactic in every sense—morale, manhood, contact, sanity—and yet, like so much else in life, took a perverse twist. The masochist in me made hay with the fact of my helplessness, and I began to fantasize during lovemaking that I was becoming a love-slave, employed by my tender friend for no purpose except sensuality, that my existence depended upon getting hard and staying hard morning and night. I focused in blind obsession upon giving pleasure, on performance, frequency, reliability—imagining her a dominatrix who found me of value only as a tongue and dildo and would kick me out into the icy dark void if I ever failed. It was kinky to be blind, though I was afraid to confide this to her. Otherwise we seemed an all-American pair, each cosying the other to bandage wounds sliced by the recent severance of twenty-five-year marriages. Her husband had been unfaithful to her, so my immobility may have attracted her. I thought I'd understood masochism psychologically before, but had never recognized a Darwinian use for it. We lived together, and my gratitude to her for taking me in remains immense.

'Twilight is a blind man's holiday,' is another well-worn proverb. In Africa and Alaska I had met ageing tribesmen with clouded eyes who could still feed themselves despite their cataracts because they knew the animals' trails and haunts, and because the animals emerged to feed at dusk and early dawn, when the sun was not yet glaring above the horizon, glinting off the hunters' milky lenses and effectively blinding them. Every day, broad daylight managed to cloud

Edward Hoagland

whatever vision I had left to the opacity of tapioca; but after sunset I'd go outside again, almost tiptoeing with a tremulous joy, and sit down in the grass, my pupils expanding as dusk fell and my cataracts lost their blocking power. As if on stolen time, I gazed at the rolling landscape, the profile of the lines of trees, the lumbering clouds. I made a point of being outside at dawn as well, when the tree trunks gleamed with dew, and in the silken demi-light I might see a deer toss up its white tail and hear its pounding feet, or its reedy sneeze.

Having perhaps half an hour before the sun got over the horizon and blotted out my acuity, I invested hope and energy in these early mornings, remembering those old Indian hunters on the margin of blind destitution, who might have to make do with the threadlike outline of that deer in order to shoot a month of meals, though the moment could be prolonged by a dark rainstorm, if it was morning, or by the rising of the moon at night. Like a bug's antennae, my hands and ears sought clues, feeling the gusts of wind and hearing them, as I fingered the white flowers of wild-carrot, orange hawkweed, tigerish lilies. I couldn't drive a car, hustle a buck, smile at my good buddies, but I still had these sighted interludes, and days full of Chopin and Schubert, Arrau and Rubinstein. Life for a while could continue to be heaven on earth, as I had always believed, enhanced by telepathy as my eyes flagged.

The important thing was to avoid being deranged by talk-radio and other 'hosts'. Week by week, their garish, chameleon pleas for applause and rancid false laughter, their acrid logic, their make-nice appeals to the ecumenical piety of chuckling greed or boob-ogling, festered like a boil that never seeps away and heals. I knew that the remedy for deep-seated grief was to involve oneself with others, and I was doing a bit of that. I'd always been a listener, even an expert listener, because of how hard it was for me to talk. But if you have to walk two miles to get to town and can't read people's faces when you get there, you're less convincing than a more self-centred, sighted person. Your face goes wooden from the lack of give-and-take with other faces, and your companion, distracted by your blindness, cannot seem to lose himself in talking to you. Also your limited intake of what is current on the streets and on TV and in the newspapers, your wistful indrawn circumstance of concerns and your bumbling preoccupation with Memory Lane make you a less engrossing listener than somebody whose problem is just that he can't talk.

I was having trouble finding a surgeon who would risk rupturing my retinas while operating on my cataracts. One bright doctor on Park Avenue told me it could be 'a Pandora's box', with multiplying disasters; I should wait till I was so old I was 'coughing and bent over'. Another personable physician with a high reputation, near Fifth Avenue, kept referring to 'technical problems' regarding the prospects for surgery and would venture no prognosis. Maybe it was better to be content with a quarter-of-a-loaf, he said. Another spoke to me with a tape recorder on—he sat by the microphone—though he took painstaking photos of my retinas, perhaps as what is called 'defensive medicine'.

Hooded like a hostage, I examined my dilemma with a teary nostalgia for lesser troubles, feeling my way along the walls that hemmed me in. Then I heard about a woman surgeon who was said to be both creatively brave and cautious. I made an appointment, and, dressing carefully in a red turtleneck pullover and a blue blazer (and carrying my best book along as an offering), I went to see her. By this time I needed to squint in order to look just half a dozen feet ahead.

'You can't see!' she exclaimed immediately, when I sat down and showed her how close I had to hold a magazine. After putting in the drops and situating me in the examining chair, she said, 'We ought to operate. How soon can you do it?' Later she explained that eyes with retinas as frail as mine often fooled the ophthalmologists because an early stage cataract's effect on the patient's already bad vision was cataclysmic, whereas they could still see in and thus assumed that he or she should be able to see out, unless retinal deterioration was the real problem.

She had small confident hands and practical-looking glasses. After my operations, I thought of her romantically as Athena, the rescuer of heroes on the plains of Troy, but at first impression she reminded me of the 'A' student at a university who outperforms the males but disarms their usual resentment of a woman of studious appearance who does exceptionally well by being attentive, perceptive, efficient, unobtrusive and sympathetic, avoiding any hint of superiority or grandiosity. I trusted her, in other words, and could imagine her diminutive fingers slicing through my corneas and guiding a micro-knife into my eyes.

With nothing to lose, in any case, I soon found myself lying under a partial anaesthetic in a crowded operating room in a New York hospital, hearing conversations but recognizing only light and dark, as various mechanisms and instruments were lowered over me. A nurse said to another that she had 'hit the jackpot today, doing all eye operations'. I wondered if she was speaking with irony. Then my physician entered, happily chatting with an ophthalmological resident whom she was training. Their bubbling reminded me of sociable hours in my childhood when I'd overhead two women preparing salad, say, for a church supper.

I was naked under a paper sheet with an anaesthetic needle taped to a vein in my wrist and oxygen being piped to my nostrils; and after an interval I heard her interrupt her companionable chatter to the young resident with a pregnant pause, and then the joyous words, almost whispered: 'It's *breathtaking*, isn't it, when it goes as perfectly as that? I love it.'

'Yes,' the student said, having watched her deftly extract the clouded lens from its filmy capsule in my left eye by a new technique called *capsulorhexis*, and now insert a plastic one of sculpted specifications that had been manufactured in Bellevue, Washington, delicately into its place. But a minute later the student added, 'Oh, the lens fell on the floor.'

'That's the old lens. No harm. We don't need that,' my saviour answered, mostly for my benefit, as I drifted off to sleep.

I woke up a couple of hours later in a chair in a large room full of hernia patients who were also waking up and about to go home. My doctor, in her bluestocking street clothes, walked through to make sure that I was out of the woods, feeling buoyant because she had performed her morning's string of operations well. She reminded me that she would take the bandage off my eye in her office the next day. With one eye covered and the other still clouded by its cataract, I was led back to our hotel by Trudy, my Significant Other, in a precariously optimistic state of shock.

At eight o'clock the next morning I was in appropriately groggy pain, half-sedated, half-elated, when the doctor's maid—who was both pitying and accustomed to the sight of early-morning walking wounded—let me into her brownstone. The second floor was for patients. There was a properly dim, old-fashioned and functional examining office, but the waiting room was her drawing room, with a red-velvet, leathery, sumptuous Persian-rug decor, tall books in a breakfront, silk-screen portraits of falcons, and folding doors and a chandelier.

I was early, as usual—another proof to my teasing surgeon of how unmacho I was—and she left her coffee in the dining room downstairs, which was enlivened with uncaged grey African and green Amazonian parrots, to come and unbind my wounded eye. My stoicism of the pre-op period had evaporated: it felt as though I had run my eye into a stick. I was querulous and flinchy.

My enthusiastic, inspired surgeon mocked and praised me. 'What a fussbudget! But *excellent,* excellent. Your eye is excellent,' she exclaimed, peering with her powerful mini-light inside. It was her favourite word, as I discovered during the ensuing weeks, overhearing many other people being examined as I sat on the sofa in the waiting room.

She prescribed drops to prevent infection or any glaucoma type of damage to the optic nerve, and gave me an eye-guard for sleeping, in case I accidentally socked or rolled over upon the eye. Though most doctors wait at least six months to remove the cataract in the patient's second eye, she decided we were on a roll and said we should go ahead and do it in three weeks. Under my gimpy, grouchy air of extreme infirmity I was swelling with cheerfulness, and agreed. To amuse me further (knowing my interest in animals), she told me the gelatinous fluid she'd injected underneath my cornea to cushion it during the operation was obtained from roosters' combs.

Before that first operation, she had asked if I would prefer to be twenty-twenty without glasses when she was finished, or a bit near-sighted, as I was used to being, which was better for reading. With the implants, she could determine the result. I naturally answered that I'd like to experience perfection, to see like an airplane pilot in my sixties. But now, Athena-like, she told me casually that she had decided not to give me twenty-twenty vision; she had sewn in plastic that would assure me only twenty-forty—'better for readers'—because bookish people 'feel confused' if in late middle age they are suddenly endowed with pilots' eyes.

This peremptory decision, overruling my romantic notion of being gifted with eagle eyes, irritated me only slightly because I was so grateful to her and because I remembered with a kind of fond awe the public health nurses I had travelled with as a journalist in Alaska, who often held a life-and-death power in the isolated villages they served. A woman deathly sick was likely to receive urgent sisterly care, but with a man the question was more whimsical. If he was dirty and crude and, whatever his age, had no 'cute' aspects, he might languish like a prisoner of war, scarcely attended to until death took him. But if he was appealing in some way, whether by being brave or dignified or funny—if he had either youth or presence—the nurses would exert themselves intensely, even affectionately to help him, while seldom masking the enjoyment that flexing their power gave them.

When the doctor took off my bandage, there was no *Eureka, I can see!* because I'd never been stone-blind. Instead, just an abrupt, astounding discovery of how bright light actually is. Not the beauty— the *brightness* of the world. My eye squinted and winced, shutting out most of the sights now hammering at the door. Limping away from her office, I believed her when she'd said that the vision in my left eye had been restored. Yet the stairs, kerbs, cars and rushing strangers on the sidewalk, and all the lettering or numerals mapping the metropolis were hardly less of a problem. I reeled, I wobbled as I walked. But a bulging though still tentative joy—glimpsing shards of the rich, russet stone of the nearby buildings, and slivers of eggshell-blue above that, speared by shafts of sunlight brighter than metal—threatened to capsize me even more than my staggering gait. I kept the eye four-fifths shut, rather fearfully; yet could begin to see fragments of faces, abbreviated as if by a camera's shutter.

I sat recuperating in the darkish two-room apartment on East 19th Street that I'd sub-let for the month of November, glad it was both nondescript and dark, and that the month, as well, was a dark one. White sunshine blazed fitfully through the window bars and Venetian slats. But I could take only short doses of such splendour. I made impulsive forays into the street at all hours, grabbing a look at random faces; also the scrumptious colours of food on my plate in a restaurant. Yellow squash, green peas, orange sweet potatoes, vivid chicken livers. Ochre or sandstone apartment buildings were underlined by their staccato storefronts, cherry-red, beige-and-butter, at street level; and the hauntedly nostalgic neon sign of a bar-and-grill bespoke for me more than thirty years of lonely, happy scrambling about this and other New York neighbourhoods for love and sex and conversation, for new sensations and friendship. Trudy had had to go back to her job in Vermont now that I was ambulatory, and without being unfaithful to her I began calling people with real gusto, summoning them to have lunch, supper, coffee or a drink, like Lazarus, formerly 'terminal' but now restored to life.

I was pleased, too, to come back once or twice a week to have my new friend manipulate my pupils with her magic eyedrops—exclaiming at how 'big' they got while gazing in at my retinas and fingering my brows and cheeks—as we talked about our grown children, and her parrots squawked from the floor below. The 'crush' or tropism of a patient toward a doctor who has saved that patient's life had occurred in me; and she on her side seemed to indicate that her marriage was in some sort of temporary trouble that agitated her considerably. We lingered, talking like close pals.

The second operation didn't progress quite as famously. My lens capsule tore, and she had to revert to the 'can-opener' technique to slip the natural lens out and the plastic lens in. It is called the 'can-opener' because that is what it looks like through the macro-microscope lowered on to the patient's face from the ceiling. It is an outpatient procedure, unlike those practised sixty years ago, which required the patient to lie with his head between sandbags for several weeks. Still, I twitched with discomfort, needing extra anaesthetic through the needle taped to my fist. Nor was the same note of gaiety present in my surgeon's voice. And the resident apprentice who was observing the operation, a young man, sounded sulky in response. She was displeased with her luck at *capsulorhexis*—she told me later that her average rate of success at doing it was about fifty per cent, which made her performance with my two eyes typical—but that

Edward Hoagland

elegance, not my basic vision, was all that was at stake. The resident, she said, had been sulky because she hadn't allowed him to poke the long main anaesthetic needle into the depths of the socket of my eye, after the preliminary fist-stuff had taken effect, as student physicians observing an eye operation are usually permitted to do as a matter of politesse. She'd told him instead (as I was glad to hear, lying on the table) that 'this is a well-known writer'. She told me that she had finessed the previous resident—the young woman—in this regard by the fact that a charity patient was next in line, whom the resident would have a free hand with. So they'd simply chatted through the moment when she did the deep needle-stick behind the eye (patients are completely unaware of it) herself.

I was more than usually fearful of being mugged, or suffering any other violent tumble on the street, because a blow on the head might unstring the back of my eyes. Yet I forgot this kind of trouble when I looked up to see an aluminium plane banking toward LaGuardia under the ripped, scudding clouds, as dusk began to sparkle. People were suddenly souls, not blurry undersea shapes, and in my gluttony of walking I wandered into a print shop, squinty, stumbly, one rainy day, and saw my first museum art in a year and a half. Titian and Tintoretto—literally, heaven on earth. I sang hymns on Sunday at St George's church and sat in various local caravanserais feasting my eyes on the faces, the sunshine spilling over the plane trees outside, a prismatic dry-cleaner's sign across the street, the cello curve of a woman's hips. Actual sex, money, fame, advancement meant next to nothing to me compared to what I had gained, and I watched street folk foraging in ashcans with less pity for them just because they could see. The hell with what you had to eat, if you could see.

My savvy surgeon told me to lift nothing heavier than five pounds lest the pressure spring my retinas, but I assumed that masturbation wouldn't do this; it was the one 'blind' thing I did. Otherwise my mind shouted, *Look at the lights! Look at the sky!* The doctor had warned me I'd eventually lose my sight again, but the jewelled bridges with their lyre-like cables crossing the East River knocked me over just as they had when I'd lain on my back in my

parents' sedan at the age of four or five. At noontime at Gracie
Mansion, near my doctor's office, the East River trumpeted with blue
and pewter sliding water, curling Hellgate currents, and muscly clouds
filling the sky, all of which upped my exuberance when I went to see
her, and made us sometimes chatter into her lunch hour after the eye
exam was over.

While blind, I'd discovered how few people of either sex will
tolerate expending time on the handicapped—they're gripers,
needy, uninformed, self-absorbed, living in the past. The child's game
where someone pretends to be blind is one of the sexiest known and,
carried to the teens, you could feel a buttock or a breast quite
innocently while controlling the girl's progress, making her stumble,
then saving her from a fall, until you gave her permission to open
her eyes and you played at being helpless. But, metaphorically, 'blind'
means ignorant of basic facts, a sucker in business, politics, a
cuckold in love, the prey of real-estate or stock-market sharks,
unresponsive to the misery of troubled friends; and in real life it costs
jobs, avocations, the very heart's warmth of seeing faces. Now,
abruptly, after paying a clever lady $5,200 to stick a knife into my
eyes (the hospital and anaesthetist tripled the bill), I was liberated.
Not just returned to the *status quo ante*, as any heart or cancer
sawbones may contrive to do in roto-rootering your plumbing, but
given plastic eyes that, too good to be true, took in more than ever
before. Old body, new orbs. I was ebullient, standing straighter,
nervous energy alight, paying intense attention as if to make up for
lost time.

The blue dawn, the golden noon, even the neon lights riveted
and bewitched me. Morning, noon and night I was gazing at dear
acquaintances in Irish pubs and Italian or Chinese restaurants, in
wooden booths in nosh-and-schmoozing joints. I positively loved my
white potatoes, earthy meat loaf, red ketchup. I adored the foam on
the beer, the bubbles in ale and the checkered tablecloth.

But my friends, whom I hadn't accurately observed in several
years, looked not just older but sadder, cudgelled and beat-up. I was
supremely happy, while they who had been window-shopping,
movie-going, taking in a thousand sights during my blind times,

seemed to testify that exuberant joy in the world was wrong-headed and going to be short-lived. Was there something they knew that I didn't; or was it the other way around? Did the eyes not really matter except as a baseline? Was happiness in the long run entirely internal, grounded in a stew of genes, hormones, childhood 'conflict resolution', careerism and consumerism? Had the visible world, God's greenery, so little to do with it? The sudden elevation of my spirits was obviously because of the freakish salvation I had undergone—but did the eyes have so meagre and ambiguous an input for everybody else?

My effervescence cheered everybody up for the space of a chat. What my friends wanted, when I asked, was a partner to confide in and grow old with, a nest egg in the bank, and a feeling that their lives had registered on other people affectionately and with a watermark of honour; that they had walked a road and not a treadmill. OK and Amen. But Emerson in *Nature* suggests that there is more, speaking of becoming 'a transparent eye-ball...part and particle of God'. He also writes: 'In the woods, we return to reason and faith. There I feel that nothing can befall me in life—no disgrace, no calamity (leaving me my eyes), which nature cannot repair.' I felt almost that way in the city too, but in due course got one of my former students to carry my suitcase to the bus station and put me, still fragile, on the bus to Vermont.

We pulled out of the Port Authority bus terminal an hour after dusk. Several statuesque black prostitutes were standing shoulder to shoulder in the midst of the stream of traffic like newsboys offering their wares—dresses lowered to their waists. The driver shook his head as we headed for all-white Vermont. The city, the universal city, lent me its last lurid strings of lights.

Back in Bennington, I groped ecstatically for a realignment with the scenery I had been missing: with Mount Anthony, the little corrugated, wooded, cavey peak that overlooks the town, as well as with the sensuous roll of the field outside my window, and the granite ridge of the Green Mountains that invigorates the view to the east. Then there were the locust, ash and maple trees, the blue spruces, white birches and red-barked pines, the deer wintering in the dogwoods, the hungry possum nibbling seeds under a bird-feeder, the startling glory of a skunk's white wedge of fur in a shaft of faint light from the moon—plus things that had always bored me, like moving headlights on a road across the valley or tardy fog at ten a.m.

The faces in Bennington, including Trudy's, seemed quite new. I had no memory of them before I'd become partially blind, so I didn't see the perspective of how life had battered them, just the novelty of how they looked. It was curious to see the town, too—the Legion Hall, the post office, the taco joint, the rest home, the supermarket mall—all of which I had been driven by a hundred times without seeing a thing. How pretty the old church was where Robert Frost is buried! And down below, the town nestled in the hills the way a New England village is supposed to. Only closer could you see the boarded-up factories and the peeling, boxy houses that filled a dingy little cross-grid nearby.

Stumbling with Trudy's two small grandchildren over the snowdrifts on Main Street to get to the Bennington Steak House, I felt the twin reactions one has to a New England winter—that it's awfully repetitive, one snowstorm on the heels of another and nowhere new to go; yet what delight to hold the children by the hand, with the pink light of the street lamps spilling on the snow. Naturally, Trudy was alert to signs that I might have sought refuge with her merely while I'd been incapacitated. I did my best to let her see that this was not the case. □

The Coasts of Bohemia

A Czech History

Derek Sayer

Derek Sayer presents a history of the Czech people that is also a remarkably original history of modern Europe, told from its uneasy center.

"**A daring and exciting book, energetically and beautifully written, and complexly conceived.**"—*Kirkus Reviews*

Cloth $29.95 £21.95
ISBN 0-691-05760-5

The Knotted Subject

Hysteria and Its Discontents

Elisabeth Bronfen

Elisabeth Bronfen reveals the continuing relevance of a disorder widely thought to be a romantic formulation of the past. Through a fascinating rereading, she develops a new concept of hysteria, challenging theories linking it to dissatisfied feminine sexual desire.

"**A brilliant volume.**"
—Sander L. Gilman

"**A truly pathbreaking book.**"—Slavoj Zizek
Paper $19.95 £15.95
ISBN 0-691-01230-X

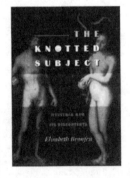

Fantasies of Salvation

Democracy, Nationalism, and Myth in Post-Communist Europe

Vladimir Tismaneanu

Eastern Europe has become an ideological battleground since the collapse of the Soviet Union. Vladimir Tismaneanu traces the intellectual history of this struggle in a vivid, forceful style.

"**Vladimir Tismaneanu dissects once more with characteristic precision, subtlety, and verve, the quickly changing body of Eastern Europe.**"
—Andrei Codrescu
Cloth $29.95 £21.95
ISBN 0-691-04826-6

PRINCETON UNIVERSITY PRESS

AT FINE BOOKSTORES OR CALL 800 777 4726 • HTTP.//PUP.PRINCETON.EDU

MARTHA GELLHORN
Nicholas Shakespeare

Martha Gellhorn wrote frequently for *Granta* in the 1980s when, late in her life, she re-established her reputation as one of the century's best reporters. She died on 15 February 1998, aged eighty-nine.

'What you and I see as a lie, in a writer is called imagination.'

I had known Martha Gellhorn ten years when she decided to investigate the plight of street children in Brazil. She was then eighty-seven years old. I put her in touch with my sister who worked with children from the Pelourinho district in the city of Salvador. On the eve of her flight, Martha sent me a fax:

WHERE ARE YOU? I AM DESPERATE. UNTIL NOW NOTHING FROM YOUR TELEPHONE, NOT EVEN A FAX WHINE. EVERY NUMBER YOU HAVE GIVEN ME FOR AMANDA IS WRONG. I HAVE BEEN WASTING TIME AND MONEY TO GET A DULL MALE VOICE SAYING HELLO HELLO HELLO AND THAT'S IT. I LEAVE ON FEB FOUR FOR ANGRA. I HAVE NO OTHER CONTACT IN ALL BRAZIL EXCEPT AMANDA. HAVE A HEART. GET THIS RIGHT FOR ME.

JUST BECAUSE YOU ARE FORTUNE'S FAVOURED KID DOESN'T MEAN ALL GOES LIKE CLOCKWORK FOR EVERYONE, YOU OAF. HELL, WHAT SHALL I DO? DESPERATELY AND ALSO VERY IRRITABLY, MARTHA.

One of Martha's blind spots was her inability to see how tyrannical she could be. She told the writer Sybille Bedford, severing their close friendship of thirty years: 'You're an awful bore, Sybille. I'm fed up with you.' As a child she had learned a thing or two from her German governess who chased her round the kitchen table in St Louis, so she averred, with a knife. She wrote to me once, 'I am always baffled by the idea that I am terrifying. If that's true how come I have friends?' In a moment of candour she added in a PS to another letter: 'I'm beginning to think you're right about me being terrifying. I've been terrifying by telephone to the *Daily Mail* and the *Irish Times* and I find it comes easily.'

Martha, in fact, was superhumanly irritable and at her stroppiest with women. 'Feminists nark me. I think they've done a terrible disservice to women, branded us as "women's writers". *Nobody* says "men writers" and before we were all simply writers. This "woman" tag leaves one seemingly apt only for women readers which is hardly my idea of my audience. I have slashed three of them and am about to slam a fourth, letters from idiot women wanting me to do or say or write things as a "woman writer". As you see, bad temper prevails.'

At the other end of the world, in Cape Town, I began to worry for my sister. I had telephoned her already (without difficulty) to ask if she would act as Martha's guide in Salvador. Before spending six years in the slums, she had lived in Peru with the Ashaninka Indians. Blonde, stubborn, with an instinctive concern for the underdog, she was, I realized, a younger version of Martha—of whom, it turns out, she has never heard.

'Then there's something about her you ought to know,' I warn my sister, 'but this must on no account be mentioned.'

I first met Martha Gellhorn one November evening in 1986 with her publisher, John Hatt, whom she adored not simply for resuscitating her fiction which had fallen out of print. Given his fondness for Mrs Thatcher, with whom he shared a birthday, one might wonder how he got through Martha's electric fence, but Hatt embodied self-sufficiency which was more important to her, in the end, than politics. And he was absolutely true to himself. She hated dissemblers even more than she hated bores ('I could kill them') and cooking (a regular dish was a stomach-rumbling stir-fry of tuna fish, sweet corn, condensed milk).

John Hatt also made her laugh. That evening he retold the story of how he attended a dinner party in New York after which, on the subway, he was looking at a map when a man came up and smiled and Hatt said loudly: 'I'm sorry, I always travel alone,' whereupon the man, hurt, replied: 'No need to be aggressive, but we were sitting beside each other at dinner.' This, Martha said, made her 'wake up' laughing.

She had come to her bare London flat from her cottage in Wales. There was a lightness in that room with its view, over the Edwardian rooftops of Cadogan Square, of a 'pink boudoir' sky. She sat elegant on a sofa, dressed in red, drinking whisky. I remember arched nostrils, a thin face bright with what she called her 'warpaint', eyes wide. She drew on a cigarette, encouraging me to talk, and lost herself in the listening. There was a flattering attentiveness in that expression. It made me, as it did everyone who met Martha, want to confide. I told her about the floating brothels of Iquitos and about life as a journalist behind the barbed wire of Murdoch's print plant in Wapping and she said, astonished and delighted, 'No!'

Her voice was well described as 'low, husky, Eastern-seaboard'. Something about her drawl, the way it took its time, its curious blend of American and English, inspired you to listen with the same care as you talked. 'My father never let us say "X says": that was gossip. Anything that begins with "I think", "I did" was OK.' She ground out her menthol cigarette, cast her eagle eyes from side to side. It was impossible to fathom a time when she had not known and spoken her mind.

The topics she roamed over that night included Robert Maxwell ('He wants to be Miss World'), politicians ('I don't trust politicians: there's a right or wrong according to humanity') and Evelyn Waugh ('A small and very ugly turd').

At the root of her dislike for Waugh, with whom she shared gutsy characteristics, was his treatment of her novel *Liana*. She had met him in Algiers in July 1944, at the house of her best friend, Diana Cooper. 'He read my book on a chaise longue from beginning to end and when he'd finished he didn't say a word.' She minded about her fiction.

I remember something else she said that night. I wondered if, living on her own in Wales, she was ever lonely. 'I was only lonely when I was married.'

We were a dozen or so. 'My chaps', she called us. About half her chaps were women, but she had grown up with three brothers and preferred, I think, the company of men: 'I was the ugly sister who couldn't dance, the guinea pig who was made to do things first.'

Now and then one of us slipped out of favour for non-attendance at court. She believed people unseen become curiously unloved. 'Out of sight out of mind, is it?' Several of her postcards read simply: 'Where *are* you?'

She liked to see us separately. She was discreet, 'not leaky', and unfailing in her eagerness to hear news. She was the person I wanted to tell about my travels and the first I telephoned when I heard of the Princess of Wales's car crash. She knew already, having listened at three a.m. to the World Service. Next day I took her to Kensington Palace. She was 'scarily blind' and I described the details to her: the notes on the flowers, the people kneeling with candles, a girl turning away with a tear falling from the end of her nose. Martha was mesmerized, though she could barely walk or see. 'It's all a con,' she whispered not quite softly enough. She had seen it before. 'It reminds me of Jackie. They were very similar. The horror when Jackie went off with a Greek. But Jackie had more style and she didn't want publicity. If you don't want publicity, you don't have to have it.'

I imagine Martha's life as a war zone and her as a young reporter sent to cover it. Wouldn't she be enraged by the restrictions imposed?

Not long ago, she gathered her most private letters, took them to her hilltop near Chepstow, and burned them. Like others, I pleaded with her not to. Why not, instead, restrict access for fifty years, a century? But burn them? She replied that she did not want some biographer misunderstanding the past. What I saw as a loss, she understood as an act of self-protection.

She hated not to be in control, and could be litigious. When she judged Bill Buford, then *Granta*'s editor, over-tardy in paying for a *Granta* piece, she went 'trembling with rage' to Chepstow's small claims court. 'I did say, "This time, Bill, you're not going to get away with it."' And when *Die Zeit* decided without her permission to footnote an article of hers about the Spanish Civil War (in order to explain the identity of a mysterious companion, referred to only as 'E'), she ran up £1,400 in lawyer's fees, preventing them.

The smallest thing excited her irritability. 'I should be in a jolly mood but am instead scratchy and pissed off due to BBC Radio 4 which is now reading snippets of my View book [*The View from the Ground*] in Books at Bedtime and had chosen as their reader an American with a voice of unparalleled ugliness and accent of startling vulgarity. They must know the difference between educated speech and cockney but apparently do not recognize that Yanks too have the basic difference as in all countries between educated and yobo speech. I feel outraged and humiliated and they firmly kept me away, making it clear I had no rights of supervisions or veto.

'Next: I have been taken in by a con man salesman about having my house painted with something that lasts forever, mould free. Due on July 3, they have not showed up and I find are not in the phone book. I now think it's a cowboy outfit with maybe one job lot of housepainters and a genius salesman. I'm already in for £750 advance and much more to come, so tomorrow starts the solicitor bit. How CAN life be so annoying?'

I had known Martha four years when she agreed to make a documentary on her life for the BBC. This promised to raise a few sparks. She was always refusing to do interviews and then doing them and then grumbling about how they turned out.

One day she rang up to say that I was to present and narrate the film. No need to worry about the commentary, she had composed this already.

The bludgeoned producer showed me her words, which succeeded in preserving her life as a vast blank. She might have sprung fully formed from Zeus' forehead so few details did she tolerate. There followed strenuous efforts to persuade her to incorporate more of what she called acidly 'the personal stuff': her family, her upbringing in St Louis, her friendship with the Roosevelts, her marriages. 'Everyone has parents, Martha—and your marriages are a public fact.' The efforts were futile.

'This letter concerns awful *Omnibus*. How happy we shall all be when that's out of the way.

'Now, I will NOT accept one word of the proposed stuff that you want, no parents, no marriages, no nothing. I am presented on the basis of my work and ideas/beliefs.' Furious that the editing process had removed from the script any word of her collected short novels, which were about to be republished, she was adamant that we reinstate this information. 'By the way I am myself impressed by my range both in journalism and fiction. I wrote a huge definitive piece on Eton and the Old Bailey, one year, and the fiction (and the people therein) are all over the lot.' Again, she was protective of her fiction.

She hated 'the dread *Omnibus*' when it was broadcast, although was pleased to hear from someone that it had made her appear 'rather rosy' at times: 'I hardly saw or heard it, being blurred by extreme anxiety and general shame.' She disliked in particular the bald reference we had inserted to her father and mother. 'You did not have permission to mention my parents, of course, and did so in a way that distresses me. The main good thing is that it's over and done with, quickly forgotten, and never never to be done again. Your help is truly appreciated, my honey. I just wish you hadn't leapt off on your own about my parents.'

In twelve years, this was as splenetic as she got with me. I was lucky. Her wrath could be abrupt and final. It came from the same fabric as her courage and curiosity and what others perceived as her heartlessness. 'Ernest told me once, "You like humanity, Martha, but your trouble is you can't stand people."'

Perhaps she did prefer people in the abstract. One of a stream of stories she repeated against herself related to an incident which took place on the day after D-Day. She had smuggled herself to the beach in the bathroom of a hospital ship. She was told to be useful, ordered to carry a stretcher. She started to undress one wounded soldier, all the while asking him to tell her what had happened, and was tugging at his boot when he screamed: 'THAT'S MY BLOODY FOOT YOU'RE PULLING OFF!'

So busy with her questions, she hadn't noticed: his leg was almost severed.

'She acknowledged a sense of shame, but she never learned from it,' said a woman friend to whom she described this episode. 'A sense was missing, which explained her insensitivity. She couldn't be so arbitrary about her relationships otherwise.'

After staying with Martha in Spain, the same friend sent her a frivolous thank-you note. 'I wrote a line implying that she was older than me—which she was, by thirty years.' As with Sybille Bedford, that was the termination of their friendship. If you hit a particular nerve, uttered one wrong phrase, she banished you irrevocably.

Her wrath was egalitarian. It observed no party line, rank or sex. (She once described herself to Bernard Berenson as equal parts male and female.) And yet her savagery towards those who came close could be a sign of approbation, especially with men and especially in friendship. But not in love. 'In the beam' was Martha's expression for being immobilized by passion and she did not savour the experience. She found herself caught in the beam only three times. 'Twice in my life the beam ended when they said a sentence.'

Once, when I was in the beam myself, she looked at me and said: 'I've never seen such a six-foot-two death wish. If I was you I'd fly immediately to Chile.' She was hungry to know every detail. But I was coming back from a front line that remained foreign. I could tell it frustrated her. If she wanted love to split her open, it never did.

'There were many worlds she didn't understand, which she thought she understood,' said Sybille Bedford.

When my love affair ended, Martha took this as confirmation of extreme good luck. 'I'm delighted it's over. Diana Cooper said to me on the day I broke up with Ernest, "You'll look back on this as the happiest day of your life."'

In 1930, Martha caused a scandal by living openly with Bertrand de Juvenel in Paris. Bertrand had been the stepson and lover of Colette who suggested Martha paint her eyebrows black, 'which made me ugly deliberately'. She said of the relationship: 'I regret it bitterly. My father never forgave me, or only just before he died. Everyone assumed Bertrand and I had this wonderful sexual life. I was pinched by every member of the French cabinet because, since he'd given up his wife and I was living openly as his lover and this was causing a huge scandal on both sides of the Atlantic, it was assumed that we had the hottest thing in bed since Anthony and Cleopatra. In fact, it was the opposite. But I felt sorry for Bertrand. He'd followed me all round Europe on my trips with a knapsack, a corkscrew and a bottle-opener and I felt sorry for him.'

Pity not lust got Martha into bed. 'In bed was the only time I was ever passive,' she said, rather amazed, as though discovering this as she spoke. She computed that 'ninety per cent' of her sexual life had been a waste of time, nothing. 'I thought I was frigid. I never saw a man and said "I want him". They wanted me. Eventually I said "Yes". Then I said "No". I always walked out. They knew what I was but once they got me they wanted to change me.'

She had one-night stands in the war because, she said, the men were going to be killed. 'It was my Florence Nightingale act. They so desperately wanted it. It meant nothing to me.' She had a weakness for handsome men who filled doorways. 'And if they were not politically revolting I slept with them.'

There was the artillery officer in Nijmegen, opposite Arnhem. The town was on fire. They'd pushed bodies from the rubble. They went home to their quarters and to bed. 'I didn't even know his name. I usually know their names. It was as if I had a piece of bread and he was hungry and I let him have it.'

There was the Pole in Italy, from the Carpathian Lancers. 'The beach was mined so we held hands on the basis we'd blow up together and tiptoed into the sea. We made love in the water. It was wonderful for him—but it just left me cold.'

She had a very good understanding of the game and she deployed her voice, her blonde hair ('like a wheatfield', wrote Hemingway), and her long distracting legs to play it, but ultimately she never understood male desire. 'They had to have it, but it was like going to the bathroom. Look at the animals. You see elephants mate. You see lions mate. The females are bored shitless. There's the lion trying to get it in and the lioness is running away or biting him. Sex is the big joke. I realize that now. And nobody cracks it. We spend time and energy on this for so little pleasure. All that sales talk, making us feel desirable. It's the great hideous solemnity, the doom. I thought I was singing for my supper with sex. I wanted to laugh.'

She laughed a lot during the Blitz. She had a room at the Dorchester, paid for by *Collier's* magazine, and sometimes she slept in the bath while the Free Dutch used her bed. Among the Dutch was a man who was dropped into occupied Holland wearing a dinner jacket so he could infiltrate the Germans at a smart party and then return. 'The war was cold, hungry, horny.' The waiters at 'the Dorch' wore grimy jackets because there was no soap and dished up sandy bread and a dollop of jam which tasted as if made from boot polish. She remembered how angry everyone was with Loelia, Duchess of Westminster because she had two eggs and made a cake which she ate all by herself.

'It was a time of laughter, hysterical or not, but laughter as well as hunger. We'd lie on the roofs watching the bombs because it was safer than in the Turkish baths and drink miniature gin bottles given to us by Mr Gilbey who was an Air Raid Warden. And laugh. Coming back from Italy four of us had to lie down on a loose bomb flap because we'd have been sucked out. And we laughed the whole way.'

What most of us think and keep to ourselves, Martha said. 'I've never been any different my whole life,' she wrote to me. She behaved at eighty-nine as she behaved at fourteen, the age at which she composed these verses at John Burroughs School in St Louis:

'Peace! do not mourn the dead,
They're in a happier land,' I said
And be a man! (yes, be a man)

But when to me great sorrow came
It seemed the case was not the same
Forsooth, why should *I* be a man? Why? Why?

She needed to be alone to write. 'I always live alone to work, cannot do it otherwise except as total immersion.' She was not especially happy on her own. 'Life in the sun would be the best life, the only life for me for writing and well being. If only there was someone at pm. for talk, jokes, drinks.' But her loneliness was her own choice: neither was she happy in a relationship. The kitchen of life, the discussions over electricity bills and dentistry, plunged her into a Greek rage.

She was at her happiest striding out alone on a journalist's cause. The Spanish Civil War, the liberation of Italy, Israel, Russia, Poland, Vietnam. This is what turned her on.

In 1989, when I was editing the books pages of the *Daily Telegraph*, I persuaded her to become our thriller-reviewer. Thrillers, for Martha, were parables of good versus evil and not boring. 'I stuff my imagination on novels that nobody has ever called art,' she wrote passionately in their defence. 'They are pure unadulterated story-telling...Unless the reader is compelled to turn the pages, *what next, what next*, all is lost.'

Every couple of months, until she lost her eyesight, she grudgingly apportioned one, two or an exceedingly rare three stars. Mostly, she preferred to award half a star. She warned: 'I am finicky about my writing, even when it is brief and hardly world shaking.' A progress report attended each batch. 'I will not read Ludlum for love or money. The Deighton is a mess. He ought to be ashamed. Surely he has enough cash in the bank not to rehash badly his other books. Another is unreadable. I've found one that rates one star...'

Another time she wrote: 'I am trying to read a book that looks as if it might be a winner but am defeated by the print. The publisher is a shit.'

In 1990, under cover as the *Daily Telegraph*'s thriller reviewer, Martha smuggled herself into Panama. She had been snorkelling in Belize, where she was trying to write a novel, when she decided to chuck it in ('if it bores me it cannot be good') and tackle the scandal of the American invasion. 'I mean to go to Panama when the troops have left...Nobody there but the natives, like going to the Eichmann Trial after the world press had departed. This is for me a duty trip, I guess, the sense that as long as I am around I have to keep on with the record, how things really are, as near as I can find out.'

She asked me to send her a To Whom It May Concern letter. 'You know the form, "the bearer, MG, is our special correspondent and any courtesies extended to her will be appreciated". That kind of thing. I think a well-known rightish paper would be the best camouflage for me as I poke into the underside of totally illegal invasion.'

I heard nothing until one day there arrived a postcard of skyscrapers. The caption read: *The banking quarter in Panama City.* On the back she had scribbled a note. 'You'll be pleased to hear that *nothing* has happened to this. On the other hand the story is fascinating.'

She was then eighty-one.

Six years after Panama, Martha read reports of destitute and defenceless little girls, 'killed as casually as if they were rabbits with myxomatosis'. Throwing herself into the cause of Brazilian street children, she flew to Salvador.

For a fortnight, my sister acted as her fixer and guide. The children opened up to her, a convicted child-killer was tracked down for her to interview. In the evening she relaxed with a talking book beside the pool in white lycra hot pants and low-heeled sandals. She also found time to snorkel.

Far from biting off her head, she decided my sister was a saint. ('Compared with you, she's a model of selflessness.')

Instead, her accumulated wrath found a target in the form of poor Colonel Paraiso, a former chief of the state police and literary man who served on the board of my sister's project. One day he invited Martha and Amanda to lunch at the Tempero de Dada. He was under strict orders from Amanda to say nothing, but as they sat down in the restaurant he could not contain his excitement. He turned to Martha and with the broadest of smiles said, 'Oh, I'm *such* a fan of Ernesto!'

In a Borges riddle to which the answer is 'knife', the only word that may not be used is 'knife'. Practically everything Martha did was more incredible to her than being the third wife of Ernest Hemingway. For eighty-four of her eighty-nine years she succeeded in not being married to him. 'To be lumbered with that fucking name...' Yet in some way Hemingway, the great unmentionable, is Martha's 'knife'.

'Of course, you can see why I am maddened by the link to Hemingway,' she wrote during 'the dread *Omnibus*' period. 'The very idea that being married to him was the most important action of my life is enough to make me want to scream. How can I lay this bloody ghost? Surely not by an autobiog. But since I now have a lot of time, due to a secretary on Thursdays, I do fiddle with such a book. I've begun by explaining why autobiographies should NOT be written.'

She did not have a good word to say about Hemingway, except that he had changed English literature a bit. He prided himself on his bullshit detector. Hers was stronger. It prevented her from writing fiction as good as his, but it made her the better reporter.

The meeting between reporter and novelist in Sloppy Joe's bar, Key West, revealed to each a heady possibility. It was the inevitable attraction of opposites. 'Just at the point when I wanted to kill him he made me laugh,' said Martha. 'He could be charming. In the company of his next wife, he told Leonard Bernstein, "Martha is the bravest women I have ever met." Lenny told me: "I didn't see how you could have married him. Now I don't see how you could have not."'

She wrote to Eleanor Roosevelt about meeting the barefoot Hemingway at Sloppy Joe's and how he was a storyteller which is forgiveable in a writer. 'So even then I must have known.' She was

Martha Gellhorn with Ernest Hemingway in 1941

vulnerable to storytellers. She spoke the truth more or less when she said: 'People can tell me anything and I'll believe them because I don't lie. I never lie. I can't, and it's all because of vanity.'

Had both had less pride they might have been able to learn the best of each other's craft. Instead, by seeking to complete themselves each devoured the other. In her view, he became a phoney and a liar, so inimical to her reporting instincts. And she, in her turn, lacked his understanding of people without which she could never match him as a novelist. Both behaved badly.

She resented him enormously and forbade any public coupling of their names. But to her friends she talked of him incessantly. Sometimes I wrote it down.

'He chased me. I didn't want to marry him. If I'd said "No", he'd have killed me. When I told him, "What will happen when I don't love you?" he was *déraciné*.' Her parents were against it. 'After he proposed my mother came and said: "You can't do this, you're happy. You should just live together." My mother was the only person he always liked—until he sent her the manuscript of *The Old Man and the Sea* as a gift and she sent it back saying sweetly thank you, she'd already read it, in book form. He never spoke to her again. I think he was insane, I really do.'

After Spain, they lived in Cuba. This was the most prolific writing time of her life and his. 'He'd get up early, reread everything he had written to get back into it. At the end he had very little time left for writing. He'd write till one o'clock and think he'd done a good day if he'd written three hundred and fifty words. Five hundred was very good. Meals happened when he decided. He wasn't a great conversationalist. He'd eat lunch in silence, then go out with a gun to kick up a guinea fowl. In the evening he'd exercise, play tennis— also in silence, he wasn't very good—or fish. Then he'd read. He was widely read, but didn't let his literary reading affect his writing. He read anything that didn't interfere with his style, like *The History of the Peninsular War*. He had a requisite for genius, which Lenny Bernstein also has, which was a perfect memory. He didn't take notes because he could remember all he needed, a hill, the soil, the trees in the soil. He used to read me what he'd written early on. He was writing *For Whom the Bell Tolls* [dedicated to her] and I thought it was dreadful, so he didn't go on with that.

'He saw no one from Monday to Saturday and never answered the phone. On Saturday night he'd go and get drunk and on Sunday afternoon he'd have people round to tell stories to. He told them with a lot of swearing. He liked chaps. He wasn't gay, not a shred of that, but women frightened him. He wasn't talented for intimacy.

'Then when he'd finished a book he'd drink because he had nothing to do and he'd go fishing for Nazi submarines. I had to get Roosevelt to give him a machine-gun—which he sent, being an adventurer. Ernest claimed he found a submarine, but I didn't believe him.'

She could not be herself in the blaze of that light, but she learned an enormous amount from Hemingway about 'the painstakingness' of writing.

'He was a complete egotist, but he did liberate English prose from mandarins like Henry James and Edith Wharton. He freed everyone into being able to write about what they felt. After Ernest it was possible to use ordinary words. He only used the words he knew, but he had this poetry. Plainspeak and cadence. He didn't get it from anywhere, he got it from himself. He said to me, "We're just sitting cross-legged in a bazaar and if people aren't interested in what we're saying they'll go away."'

With astonishment, Martha came to understand that he was jealous of her. He was nine years older, the most glamorous writer in the world—at Bryn Mawr her generation had adopted *The Sun Also Rises* for their Bible—and he was jealous. 'After twenty years I realize that's what it was. It was like being jealous of Mickey Spillane. He hated the fact I earned my living. He wanted every other writer dead. He told me Dos Passos was a shit, and he never wrote a puff for any younger novelists. So far as he was concerned there was only him. When I showed him *Liana* he said, "Not bad for a Bryn Mawr girl."'

In the meantime, he wrote to his mother saying *Liana* was better than anything he had written.

One day in 1941 Hemingway uttered the sentence which ended their marriage. 'I'd known him four years when I realized he was a liar. It was shocking. Mr Josie, who'd run the bar in Key West, came to see him in Havana. He saw Ernest only once because Ernest was writing and then Josie got so drunk he was arrested and put in a straitjacket and he died. Ernest said: "I couldn't see him because Marty wanted to spend the day on the boat." It was a lie. I never wanted to go on the boat. Anything uncomfortable he offloaded with a lie. He lied about everything.'

Again she wrote to Eleanor Roosevelt. 'What you and I see as a lie, in a writer is called imagination.'

If one was tough, one might understand this as a defence of her own failure to write persuasive fiction. She took a long time to accept that the virtues which made her journalism so good are, in novels, a vice. It was not enough to be there. One could go further and say that her fiction is pinioned by the reporter's topicality. Unable to transcend her own experience, she doomed her characters to enacting her political cosmology. Always there is the plucky liberal heroine, usually a black Martha, and then there are the bigots who stumble around in the darkness of her devising until she reveals the political errors of their ways and they're punished with a genuine contempt for their failing.

In the same way, she spoke scathingly of what she called Hemingway's 'mythomania'. 'Having lived with a mythomane,' she wrote, 'I know they believe everything they say; they are not conscious liars, they invent to increase everything about themselves and their lives and *believe* it.'

Once in Spain she and Hemingway rode up a hill on horseback and came down again in a makeshift armoured car. 'That was that,' she said. 'But to him, when he described it there were machine-gun bullets and one as I remember that came in and ricocheted around. But it was shit. Not a bullet. I was so baffled and stunned I didn't know what to say. If you say to a mythomane, "But I was there!" they just look at you like you're a halfwit. It's *you* who were wrong. It was terrible having me around, my eyes open, my mouth open.'

She noted with mounting exasperation how in his novels he had to be the hero. 'When you're daydreaming as a child you're Joan of Arc or Richard Coeur de Lion: that's the one pleasure of childhood. But it's supposed to change. Ernest always cast himself in a bigger light. He didn't mythomane down, only up. He had an accurate

231

memory of things you *don't* mythomane about: scenery, places, names. That worked very well. The scenery was exact and correct, but the hero striding through it was larger than life. Finally, in *The Old Man and the Sea*, he was a mixture of himself and Christ.'

It was the same in bed. There was no question of the earth moving for Martha. 'He was meant to be a great lover. Absolute balls. He was a rotten lover. Sex for him was a necessity, like having vitamins. He took it regularly every night, but he gave no thought to the woman's pleasure.' She believed he had been a virgin when he married. 'He had to marry his women to have sex. I'm convinced he only went to bed with five women: the women he married and one other I know of. And he was no good at it.'

A year or two ago, Martha saw herself portrayed in a television drama. 'We're making love and his friends come in and say, "Hem, we're off to the front," and I creep naked out of bed after him and say, "Hey! Wait for me." It's not just the plot and the lines that are wrong, it's the facts. He never wanted to go to the front.'

It was Martha who bullied a reluctant Hemingway to cover the D-Day landings. 'We were living in Cuba and not going to the war. I thought this was wrong.'

Out of revenge, she believed, he took her job at *Collier's*. The magazine, able to accredit one correspondent only, chose Hemingway. He flew to Europe via Roald Dahl, the Defence Attaché in Washington. She meanwhile had to sail for fifteen days on a freighter loaded with explosives. They saw each other in the Dorchester. He had spent one day covering the D-Day landings and hared back, never having actually reached shore. She had been aboard the hospital ship with the troops. When he saw her come in, he said: 'Killed any Germans, Mookie?' She went and slept in his room and locked the door.

Later, she saw a doodlebug 'like a child's toy across the sky' dash into the Cumberland Hotel. Hemingway came out of the lift with his swarm of acolytes and said to her: 'So it missed you, then. I wish it had hit you.' Martha said, 'This was taboo: to talk about casualties, and to wish harm.'

She left him and asked for a divorce. She read about her divorce in *Time*. She never heard from him except once. He sent back her stuff in a metal box, unwrapped, with everything shattered and he made her pay for it 'when I had taken nothing'. When she complained he wrote to say, indignantly, that his new wife had packed the box and Martha's complaint was an insult to Mary.

'He was always crazy, but after he was wrongly diagnosed and they put electrodes on his head, he lost his memory and that made him suicidal. He had often talked about how he would do it. He'd point a shotgun at his mouth and pull the trigger with his toe. He did it at the top of the stairs so she would see.'

'What did you feel when he killed himself?'

'Nothing.'

She had demanded a divorce to be free of him and return to who she was. 'I just wanted my name back on my passport.'

The Gellhorns, not Hemingway, had made Martha who she was. In 1899, her father George Gellhorn arrived in St Louis from Breslau after spending two years as a ship's doctor in the Far East. He had an introduction to the top internist, whose daughter he fell for, courted with fresh violets and married, and became the only gynaecologist in town. He set 'icily high' standards and regarded Hitler as a personal insult. From her Prussian father Martha inherited a desire to travel and an instinct for the literal truth.

Martha counted on one hand the perfect marriages she had known. 'It's as rare as a great ballerina or a novel by Tolstoy.' Her parents' marriage was one of them. 'She runs as fast to meet me as when we were first married,' said George Gellhorn. Another was the marriage of Martha's younger brother Alfred.

At her wake in March this year, Alfred spoke of the moment when his sister first registered him as a baby. He was sitting under the table when Martha dashed through the kitchen chased by their governess, Miss Peters. She stopped in her tracks. 'What's *that*?' And then, when the matter was explained, 'But mummy wasn't fat.'

Her mother, Edna Fischel, was a blue-eyed suffragette who founded the St Louis League of Women Voters. From her, Martha evolved her articulate hatred of injustice. After she left home, at seventeen, she wrote to Edna every day for several years. 'Mother thought something was wrong if Martha didn't say what a disaster something had been,' said Alfred. On 18 December 1968, Martha awarded her mother a star of survival, first class. 'This decoration is awarded for lifelong and unfailing gallantry, generosity and gaiety, with an added citation for beauty. Only grown-ups (ie 80 & over) are eligible and as the combination of required qualities is so rare this medal is bestowed for the first time in history on Edna Fischel Gellhorn on her 90th birthday.'

Maybe, said Alfred at Martha's wake, it was time to bestow this star again.

The last time I saw Martha was with my sister and two other 'chaps'. She was standing against her skyline, dressed in a red velvet pant suit and Robin Hood boots with smart pointed toes. She could no longer drink, smoke, travel, read, but she looked ravishing. She talked about her solution for Iraq (to arm the Kurds in the north and south), about the media harassment of Clinton, about the books she had been listening to. She was excited because my sister had come with a tape of *The Spy Who Came in from the Cold*. At some point she said, rather too matter of factly, 'I'm not a natural novelist because I can't invent.'

Afterwards, going down in her juddering lift, I wished I had found the courage to tell Martha that what clipped the wings of her fiction and grounded her imagination was precisely what made her soar as a journalist.

She turned from her pink skyline and said: 'And now you must all leave.'

Martha had an adopted son, Sandy. At four in the morning on Sunday 15 February 1998, he was woken at his home in the English countryside by what he thought was the cry of a strange bird. The sound went straight through him and the hair, as he says, stood up on the back of his neck. 'I'd never heard a sound like it. It was scary, but I wasn't scared.' He rose from his bed, looked over the courtyard, saw nothing. But the sound was insistent, like someone wagging a finger, saying, 'Now you remember this.' There was also a softness. 'And I love you.'

This was around the time Martha died. She was not religious. She trusted the world in front of her eyes, not any other. 'Oh, me I just want to get there, put on my mask and start swimming,' she wrote about Belize. In Brazil, she had so loved the trees near Salvador that she sought out a botanist and spent a day with him. Her last outing, four days before she died, was a visit to the Cartier-Bresson exhibition at the Hayward Gallery. The same age as the photographer, she found his work 'too arty' and criticized him for aestheticizing experience. 'It's all media hype. This is supposed to be a testament of our century, yet there's no record of human suffering.' She could not bother herself to ride the escalator down to see the Francis Bacon canvases—'so many slabs of meat at the butcher'. She said: 'Nothing interests me any more except the natural world. It has the most to teach.' At my home in Wiltshire, the snowdrops had come out. She wanted to hear about them.

On the day after her wake, as instructed, Martha's ashes were strewn on the Thames near Tower Bridge for her 'continuing travels'. Her instructions had ended: 'and if it's inconvenient, what the hell'.

'Was it an outgoing tide?' I asked her stepson.

'Oh God,' he said, 'I hope so.'   □

Pieces by Martha Gellhorn, including her reports from Germany, Cuba and Panama, were published in Grantas 10, 11, 20, 23, 32 and 42, which are all still in print. Two collections of her reportage, The View from the Ground and The Face of War, were republished this year by Granta Books.

creative camera
REVEALING PHOTOGRAPHY

Johannes Wohnseifer

'The Granta of photography' – The Guardian

Six times a year Creative Camera focuses on the images and news that inform the world of photography, interviews and reviews those who shape its landscape and provides listings of events and exhibits across the UK and around the world.

For 30 years Creative Camera has been at the leading edge of the photographic world, introducing audiences to the work of renowned figures such as Robert Frank, Martin Parr and Robert Mapplethorpe.

To subscribe today call 0171 729 6993

Or send a cheque for £24 (UK individuals)/£18 (UK students) to 5 Hoxton Square, London, N1 6NU or visit our web site at http://www.ccamera.demon.co.uk

SPECIAL OFFER – THE FIRST 100 ENQUIRERS WILL RECEIVE A FREE SAMPLE COPY OF CREATIVE CAMERA

EATING GLASS

Alfred Lawrie

Terry Cole, record-breaker

In the Montparnasse cemetery in Paris stands a marble tablet inscribed with the following words:

ALEXANDER ALEKHINE 1892–1946

CHESS GENIUS OF RUSSIA AND FRANCE

Alekhine was the world chess champion for seventeen years, and in death achieved his stated ambition of being the first and so far the only man to take his world title to the grave. He was brilliant in many spheres, fluent in ten languages, but it was to chess that he dedicated his life. Of all the great chess masters it is he, with his emphasis on forceful, aggressive strategies, who most inspired the present world champion, Gary Kasparov. At the age of seven Alekhine would pore over chess positions by candlelight in bed; at school he would be working them out in his head.

In adult life he always carried a pocket chess set, which he would study regardless of the surroundings or company. There is a story that he was once taken to the opera with Capablanca, the Cuban chess champion whom Alekhine had defeated en route to his first world title. Capablanca could not keep his eyes off the chorus line, while Alekhine could not be persuaded to lift his gaze from the chess set on his lap. He even died sitting at a chessboard, alone in a modest hotel room, annotating a variation of a Caro-Kann Defence opening.

This love affair with the chessboard looks very different in the light of a letter Alekhine wrote two years before his death to a fellow chess master, Juan Fernandez Rua. At first glance, his words sit strangely with the way he chose to lead his life.

> If, sometime, I write my memoirs—which is very possible—people will realize that chess has been a minor factor in my life. It gave me the opportunity to further an ambition and at the same time convince me of the futility of that ambition. Today, I continue to play chess because it occupies my mind and keeps me from brooding and remembering.

The noun 'game' takes the verb 'to play' and this can lead to confusion. Participation in a game is not the same thing as play, even when the two overlap. The game is a kind of ritual, with rigid rules and goals. Play as in playfulness is an outlook on life.

Sometimes a group of friends will be moved to begin a game, each dreaming of wild, audacious schemes, surprising ways of beating each other. The game will be joyful; a means for them to play against and harmlessly wallop one another. Perhaps, when they are done, they will open a bottle of whisky and the play will continue, though the game itself is forgotten.

Sometimes people are driven not by love but by boredom or frustration, and the game becomes something else: a retreat from the hardships of the world outside it.

The spirit of play is wanton, capricious, moody and hedonistic. It can motivate just about anything, from sport to music to conversation, but it can also be entirely absent from these things. This is the sense in which a game properly played involves no play at all.

In *The Guinness Book of Records* there are some individuals who have several records to their name. Most peculiar, to my mind, are the specialists in eating records, who each seem to have their own area of expertise. Peter Dowdeswell, for example, is listed as holding records for eggs, prunes and spaghetti. Reg Morris, on the other hand, has set less wholesome landmarks, holding records in the frankfurter, kipper and sausage departments.

In the field of endurance records, however, two names stand out: Terry Cole, a Londoner, and an American, Ashrita Furman. They have so many records—twenty or thirty each—that *The Guinness Book of Records* publishes only a small selection of their achievements. They have never met; they communicate by trying to break each other's records. The feats they attempt vary a great deal, and it is hard to imagine who ever conceived of some of them; the record for balancing as many milk crates as possible on the chin, for example, or carrying a brick in one hand as far as possible (the palm of the hand must be above the brick, so that it is gripped between fingers and thumb). What most of these records share, though, is an indifference to skill; most are simply tests of will and endurance.

I went to visit Terry Cole in his terrace house in East London, where he lives alone among a clutter of ornaments, certificates, trophies, and several enormous weight-training machines. He also has a small garden, which when I visited was full of milk crates. I presumed he had once balanced these on his chin.

His smile revealed a row of gold teeth, and I wondered if there was a medical reason for them.

'Oh no,' he said. 'No medical reason at all, actually. It's a British record, fourteen gold teeth. It was the idea of a manager of mine. He paid for them. Cost him six thousand pounds.'

One of the first world-record certificates Terry Cole showed me, as he started going through them, was for rolling head over heels for one mile in twenty-four minutes. I asked him to tell me about that record.

'I saw Ashrita Furman do it on the television,' he said. 'And he did in twenty-six minutes. And I thought, It's feasible to beat that. It's feasible to beat that. And, I'm lucky. Because I've got a little paved alley at the back of my house. And I practise up and down the alley. I put my motorbike helmet on. And away I go. Up and down. A bit of padding on my back. And we're kicking! I started off practising at midday, and I did that for three or four days, and I thought, No, this isn't happening, man. Your coordination goes, and it makes you ever so tired during the day. And I had other things I had to do as well. You know, I had to do my weight training, and my martial arts. Conditioning my hands. And I was, like, knackered. Totally knackered. So I thought, how do you practise and not be tired during the day? And the answer was to practise just before I went to bed. So that's what I did, for about four months.'

'I guess the attempt itself must have been sickening,' I said.

'Oh, bad news. Seriously bad news. I remember it. It was very, very horrific. It was four times around a track, and you had to concentrate on taking the bends. And people had to push me from the sides to keep me in the right direction. I was sick, bad, everything. Vomiting. The works. I was totally distorted. Focused, though. Totally, totally focused. But the last four hundred metres I was puking up all over the place. Look, [he flicked through the certificates] I've dribbled a basketball for ninety miles. That was a hard one to do.'

'What is the most horrific record you've attempted?'

'One-armed press-ups, definitely.'

'How many did you do?'

'I did eight thousand, in five hours.'

'Eight thousand?'

'Yeh. Nutty.'

'And is that record still standing?'

'No. Paddy Doyle beat me two weeks later. Done my fucking nut.'

'It must have been very annoying.'

'Yes.'

A pause.

'Why was that the hardest?'

'Because it was on one arm, basically. Yeh. That's me when I actually finished the press-ups. [He held out a photo. In it, someone was standing beside him, actually holding up his exhausted arm for him.] I was dying. You had to stay on one arm for the five hours. I was dying. The fingertip press-ups was one of the hardest as well. But I mean, *all* world records are hard. [We both laughed—he said it so seriously.] They're all hard. They're all very, very, very hard. You know. Very hard.'

'You enjoy the challenge though?'

'Yeh, I rise to the challenge. I'm a very competitive person. Very competitive. And, I haven't got nothing else to do. [A pause.] If I had a full-time job...Let's put it like this. If you take the monks, in their monasteries, they don't do anything. What do they do? They pray, and they train. All the time. That's what I do. This is *my* monastery. This is where I live.'

'Have you ever gone for a record and failed?'

'My worst one was the crawling record. But it wasn't really my fault. It started to rain, and I had to stop. I *had* to stop, it was thundering.'

'How far had you gone?'

'Eleven miles. The world record is thirty-one, a lot further. But I'd actually crawled eleven miles on my hands and knees for nothing. And I was pissed off. I was pissed off. Very pissed off.'

'I suppose crawling eleven miles is hard?'

'Oh yeh! Very hard. That's what my Powerjog is for. I could take you round this house. Every piece of equipment is for a specific job.'

I asked him what lay ahead.

'You know, I'm going to be at an exhibition at Olympia for six days, eating glass. I'm the only guy in Europe that does it. Mr Mangetout is the expert.'

'When did you start eating glass?'

'Well, I eat light bulbs. It's…I mean, I eat glass, not on a regular basis. Not on a regular basis at all. But if the work comes in, then I'll do it. It's paid work, you see. It'll be paid work.'

'And what is it like to eat glass?'

'What's it like eating glass? Awful. Yeh, really awful.'

'Does it have any ill effects?'

'No. Not really. It doesn't cut you, because you grind it very thoroughly with your teeth. As long as you grind it up for long enough, you're all right.'

'Tell me, how does it make you feel to be a world champion?'

'I am very proud of what I've achieved in my past.'

'One gets the sense talking to some athletes that their sport comes to define their life.'

'Well this is what my training does. This is what I do all day, every day. A lot of my friends say that I train too hard, I do too much. But that is a part of *me*. It's a part of my life. And when I train for a world record, I train very, very hard for the world record. And I'll keep on doing that. I mean, I'm thirty-eight years old now. I don't feel thirty-eight. And I will carry on until I drop dead. I will die of a heart attack. I know that. But as far as I'm concerned, if you want to be the best, then it's up to you. It's in your hands.'

'Do you think you have passed your peak?'

'No. No. My peak is ahead.'

'Always going forward.'

'Always. I'm a very positive thinker.'

The telephone rang, and Terry discussed his forthcoming appearance at Olympia. When he hung up, he was excited.

'Unbelievable. This other agency—because I'm the only guy that eats glass—all of a sudden, it's like everybody wants Terry Cole. He'll eat glass! They're not interested in the world records. They want me to do something totally stupid, totally bizarre, and eat glass!'

'You must have sometimes considered giving it all up.'

'Yeh, I've thought that.'

'How often?'

'Not very often. But when I get down. When I get kicked down. I get kicked down a lot, you know. I get kicked by people.'

'In your personal life, or professionally?'

A pause.

'I come across a lot of jealousy in my life. People that I meet. Competitors. Other people. And I have to keep it very, very careful in what I do and say to people. That is why I keep it very, very well under wraps what I do.'

'You mean when you're introduced to someone?'

'Exactly that. When I'm introduced to somebody. One of my mates, Barry, he'll introduce me to one of his friends, and he'll say, Oh, Terry does this, Terry Cole does that. I'm very, very shy. I'm a very shy person.'

'You don't seem shy talking to me now.'

'No. But I am if I go out. I'm not a good mixer. I'm *not* a good mixer. I know that.'

'Do you think that is connected with your sport in any way?'

'I find that when I go out socially with people, I don't have anything in common with them. I don't know what to talk about. I really...I get stuck. I get really stuck. I think, Well, OK, what are we going to talk about. I mean, I've got a few good friends. Like John, and my mate Cliff who's a drummer in a band. But when I go out with them, they really find that they talk to *me*, and they have to get a conversation out of me. But if it was left to me to talk to them, I would find it very difficult.'

A pause.

'What's the closest you've ever come to retiring?'

'Never.'

'Never?'

'Never.'

'Because you said that sometimes you get down. Do you never think of giving it up?'

'No, no, no. I get down. I get very down sometimes. I get very depressed. I mean, *now*. I mean, *now*. I'm going through such a hard time. I'm going through such a...I got a letter yesterday. Do you want to see it?'

'I don't want to pry.'

'I'll show it to you. Right. I'll show it to you. This...this came through the post to me. And still I trained.'

He held up a letter, handwritten on two sides of A4. It was from someone telling him their relationship was over.

'I'm going through a very hard—mentally—a very hard time. Because. [Pause.] I loved Susie, man. [His voice choked.] I really loved her. And she was a schoolteacher, and she...she thought she could accept the way that I am. I'm different. And now I know that she was with me because I was different. Because I was exciting to be with. Do you know what I mean? She didn't love me—she just loved what I am. And at the end of the day...you know...you still have to pick up the pieces. [Long pause.] And you know, I will still train, and I will still fight to the end. I am a fighter, I'm not a quitter. You know, I'm not a quitter. And some people find it very hard to...some of my friends. Even my closest friends. They, er, I don't know really, they...they like *parts* of me. And some people don't like parts of me. Do you know what I mean? But I'm still waiting to see, to find the friend—not a girlfriend—to find a friend, a good friend, who accepts me the way I am. You know, and I really haven't found that friend yet. I've got friends that accept parts of me. You know, that want to know about parts of me. But also, that don't want to know about other parts of me. Do you know what I mean? And you can go out and mow the lawn on a Sunday afternoon, but there's nothing clever about that. It's just doing what your neighbours do. I don't like that. I'm not that sort of bloke. You know, I'm not really the sort of bloke to get married and have a family. As much as I would like a little boy, I want someone to accept me the way that I am. You know, because I accept other people the way that they are. The way that you are.'

'Do you sometimes long to be ordinary?'

'Oh yeh. Ordinary. Yeh. Sometimes I do. But it doesn't last for long. It lasts a couple of seconds. I go, Na! That's not me. I don't *want* to be ordinary. You know, I will never be ordinary. And at the back of my mind, I always *knew* that there would only ever be one Terry Cole. Really. [Pause. Again, his voice filled with emotion.] There'll only ever be one Terry Cole. There'll be no children. There'll be no wife. There'll be no sons. There'll be no daughters. I came into this world alone. And I will die alone. One day, my friends, one of

Alfred Lawrie

my friends will come round, and—I'm sure it won't be *here*, [he gestured around the house, which he rents]—but wherever I'm living at the time. And I'll just be dead.'

'That's a very hard thing to say.'

'Yes. They'll come round one day, and I'll just be on the floor. I'll be with some weights on top of me, or...And I'll just die. And that is how I will die. I know that. [He held off tears.] That is how I will die, and I will die alone. [A pause.] But I'm *happy*, in my life. You know. I'm a happy person, yeh. Money is nothing. I don't do it for money. I've got some nice things. I've got a nice gym. And everything round here is geared for me. I *like* doing charity work. You know, when Susie was here, I burned a fifty pound note in front of her once. I said, Baby this doesn't make us happy. She was shocked. She said, What are you doing! I said, Money's nothing. Do it because you enjoy it, because you want to do it, and you want to be the best. Money is nothing. But if you want a happy relationship, money helps...'

He gets down a scrapbook. On the front, he had glued letters cut out from different colours of paper to spell the following:

THERE LIVED A CERTAIN MAN IN ENGLAND LONG AGO
WHO WAS BIG AND STRONG AND TEETH PAVED WITH GOLD.

'When I die, people will read that. People will read that. I'm preparing myself for death.'

If nobody can ever love you—because you are so different, or special—should you consider that to be a flaw within yourself? Or a flaw within every other person in the world except yourself. Or simply a flaw in the human design.

Alekhine's death did not come in happy circumstances. Living in hotel rooms, with so little money that he once complained he could not even buy a few cigarettes, his alcoholism had given him cirrhosis of the liver. A couple of days before his death, he had begged the Portuguese chess champion, Fransisco Lupi:

Lupi, the loneliness is killing me! I must live. I must feel life about me. I have already worn down the floorboards of my room. Take me to some nightclub.

Lupi obliged, and the evening lifted Alekhine's spirits. But as dawn broke the next day, his despair returned. He continued to study chess alone in his room; but now he was not being drawn by a love of the game; it was just a way of hiding from his own unhappiness. He had given more of himself to chess than any man before him, and found that the consequence of having given himself so sparingly to life was that his life now offered him nothing in return. His games will live for ever; but for the man, death, in the end, could not come too soon.

□

GRANTA

WHERE DOES WRITING COME FROM?

Richard Ford

Richard Ford

Where does writing come from? I've often been guilty of trying to answer this question. I've done so, I suppose, in the spirit André Breton must've had in mind when he wrote:

> Our brains are dulled by the incurable mania of wanting to make the unknown known.

I've done it on public stages after readings, in panel discussions with dozing colleagues, standing before rows of smirking students, at the suggestion of cruel and cynical journalists in hotel rooms at home and abroad. And I believe I can honestly say that I would never spontaneously have asked myself this question had not someone else seemed interested, or had my financial fortunes not seemed (correctly or incorrectly) tied to such speculation. I must've thought I knew the answer, or thought I didn't need to know it. Yet, once the question was asked, I've over the years taken an interest in the answers I've come up with—which is to say, dreamed up—much in the way I take interest in the progress of any piece of fiction I'm writing. This, after all, is what one does, or what I do anyway when I write fiction: pick out something far-fetched or at least previously unthought of by me, something I feel a kind of language-less yen for, and then see what I can dream up about it or around it that's interesting or amusing to myself in the hope that by making it make sense in words I'll make it interesting and important to someone else.

Plenty of writers for plenty of centuries have furrowed their brows over this question—where does it come from, all this stuff you write? An important part of Wordsworth's answer for instance was that '...good poetry is the spontaneous overflow of powerful feelings'. And I've seen no reason I shouldn't just as well get my two cents' worth down on the chance I might actually get to or near the bottom of the whole subject and possibly help extinguish literature once and for all—since that seems to be where the enquiry tends: let's get writing explained and turned into a neat theorem, like a teasing problem in plasma physics, so we can forget about it and get back to watching *Seinfeld*. And failing that, I might at least say something witty or charming that could make a listener or a reader seek out the book I really *do* care about—the one I've just written and hope you'll love.

It may be that this investigation stays alive in America partly because of that principally American institution, the creative writing course—of which I am a bona fide graduate, and about which Europeans like to roll their eyes. The institution has many virtues—time to write being the most precious. But it also has several faults, one of which is the unproven good of constantly having like-minded colleagues and compatriots around to talk to about what one is doing, as if companionship naturally improved one's important work just when one is doing it. How we do what we do and why we do it may just be a subject a certain kind of anxious person can't help tumbling to at a time in life when getting things written at all is a worry, and when one's body of work is small and not very distinguishable from one's private self, and when one comes to find that the actual thing one is writing is not a very riveting topic of conversation over drinks. Among dedicated novices, the large subject of provenance may be all we have in common and all that will pass for artily abstract speculation of a disinterested kind.

Clearly another socio-literary force which keeps the topic alive is that among many people who are not writers there's occasionally a flighty belief that writers are special people, vergers of some kind, in charge of an important interior any person would be wise to come close to as a way of sidling up to a potent life's essence. Questions about how, why, etc. become just genuflects before the medium. And writers, being generally undercharged in self-esteem and forever wanting more attention for their work, are often quite willing to become their work's exponent if not its actual avatar. I remember an anecdote about a male writer I know who, upon conducting an interested visitor to his desk overlooking the Pacific, is reported to have whispered as they tiptoed into the sacred, sun-shot room, 'Well, here it is. This is where I make the magic.'

Again, nothing's new here: just another instance of supposing an approach upon the writer will reveal the written thing more fully, more truly; or if not that then it's the old mistake of confusing the maker with the made thing—an object which may really have some magical pizzazz about it, who knows?

Considering an actual set of mechanical connections that might have brought a piece of writing from nowhere, the 'place' it resided before I'd written it, to its final condition as the book I hope you'll love, actually impresses upon me the romantic view that artistic invention *is* a kind of casual magic, one which can't be adequately explained the way, say, a train's arrival in Des Moines can nicely be accounted for by tracing the tracks and switches and sidings and tunnels all the way to its origin in Paducah.

You can—and scholars do—try to trace some apparent connections back from the finished work to the original blank mind and page and even to before that ('He used his father's name for the axe-murderer'...hmmm; 'she suffered glaucoma just like the jilted sister who became a Carmelite nun, so how can you argue the whole damn story isn't about moral blindness?'). But of course such a procedure is famously unreliable and even sometimes downright impertinent, since in the first place (and there need not be a second) such investigations start at and take for granted the existence of Des Moines, whereas for the writer (and I mean soon to abandon this train business) Des Moines is not just a city but a word that has to be not merely found, but conjured from nothing. In fact the word may not even have been Des Moines to begin with—it may have been Abilene or Chagrin Falls—but became Des Moines because the writer inadvertently let Abilene slip his mind, or because Des Moines had that nice diphthong in it and looked neat and Frenchy on the page, whereas Abilene had those three clunky syllables, and there was already a dopey country song about it. Anyway, there are at least two Abilenes, one in Texas and another one in Kansas, which is confusing, and neither has rail service.

You can see what I mean: the true connections might never really be traceable because they exist only in that murky, silent but fecund interstellar night where impulse, free association, instinct and error reign. And even if I were faithfully to try explaining the etiological connections in a piece of writing I'd done, I still might lie about them, or I might just be wrong because I forgot. But in any case I'd finally have to make something up pretty much the way a scholar does—though not exactly like a writer does who, as I said before, always starts with nothing.

I remember once a complimentary reviewer of a book I'd written singling out for approval my choice of adjectives, which seemed to him surprising and expansive and of benefit to the story. One sentence he liked contained a phrase in which I'd referred to a character's eyes as 'old': 'He looked on her in an old-eyed way.' Naturally, I was pleased to have written *something* that *somebody* liked. Only, when I was not long afterward packing away manuscripts for the attic, my eyes happened to fall upon the page and the very commended phrase, 'old-eyed', and to notice that somehow in the rounds of fatigued retyping that used to precede a writer's final sign-off on a book in the days before word processors, the original and rather dully hybridized 'cold-eyed' had somehow lost its 'c' and become 'old-eyed', only nobody'd noticed since they both made a kind of sense.

This is my larger point writ, admittedly, small, and it calls to mind the joke about the man from Alabama who couldn't understand how a thermos could keep cold things cold and hot things always hot, and expressed his wonder in a phrase akin to the title of this very essay: 'How do it know?'

Anyone who's ever written a novel or a story or a poem and had the occasion later to converse about it with an agitated or merely interested reader knows the pinchy feel that comes when the reader tries to nail down the connections *linking* the story to some supposed 'source', either as a way of illuminating the procedures that transform life to shapely art, or else of just plain diminishing an act of creation to some problem of industrial design.

In my case, this enquiry often centres on the potent subject of children, and specifically writing about children, and more prosecutorily on how it is I can write about children to such and such effect without actually having or having had any myself. (My wife and I don't have any.)

It's frequently surprising to whomever I'm speaking to that I can write persuasively about children: although the surprise is often expressed not as pure delight but in a kind of blinkingly suspicious tone whose spirit is either that I do have children (in another county, maybe) and don't want to admit it, or else that somebody in a position of authority needs to come down and take a closer look at my little minor inventions to certify that they're really as finely and truly drawn as they seem.

Myself, I try to stay in happy spirits about such questioning. Some stranger, after all, *has* or seems to have read at least a part of some book I've written and been moved by it, and I'm always grateful for that. He or she could also as easily have been watching *Seinfeld*. And so mostly I just try to smile and chuckle and mumble-mutter something about having been a child once myself, and if that doesn't work I say something about there being children pretty much everywhere for the watchful to study, and that my Jamesian job, after all, is to be a good observer. And finally if that isn't enough I say that if it were so hard to write about children I of all people wouldn't be able to do it, since I'm no smarter than the next guy.

But the actual truth—the one I know to be true and that sustains my stories—is that even though I was once a child, and even though there are a God's own slew of bratty kids around to be studied like lab rats, and even though I'm clearly not the smartest man in the world, I still mostly write about children by making them up. I make them up out of language bits, out of my memories, out of stories in newspapers, out of overheard remarks made by my friends and their kids, out of this and out of that, and sometimes out of nothing at all but the pleasurable will to ascribe something that might be interesting to a child instead of to an adult or to a spaceman or a horse, after which a child, a fictive child, begins to take shape on the page as a willed, moral gesture toward a reader. '"All I want for Christmas is to know the difference between that and which," said little Johnny, who was just ten years old but already beginning to need some firmer discipline.' Behold: a child is born.

Occasionally if pushed or annoyed I'll come right out and say it: *I make these little buggers up, that's what. So sue me.* But an odd restraint almost always makes me revert to my prior explanations. Some delicacy in me simply doesn't want to say, 'They're invented things, these characters, you can't track them down like rabbits to their holes. They won't be hiding there.' It's as though arguing for invention and its fragile, wondrous efficacy was indelicate, wasn't quite nice. And even though arguing for it wouldn't harm or taint invention's marvels (we all know novels are made-up things; it's part of our pleasure to keep such knowledge in our minds), still I always feel queasy doing it—not like a magician who reluctantly shows a rube how to pull a nickel out of his own ear, but more like a local parish priest who upon hearing a small but humiliating confession from a friend, lets the friend off easy just to move matters on to higher ground.

Wallace Stevens wrote once that 'in an age of disbelief...it is for the poet to supply the satisfactions of belief in his measure and his style'. And that takes in how I feel about invention—invented characters, invented landscapes, invented breaks of the heart and their subsequent repairs. I believe that there are important made-up things that resist precise tracing back, and that it's a blessing there are, since our acceptance of them in literature (acting as a substitute for less acceptable beliefs) suggests that for every human problem, every insoluble, every cul-de-sac, every despair, there's a chance we can conjure up an improvement—a Des Moines, where previously there was only a glum Abilene.

Frank Kermode wrote thirty years ago in his wonderful book *The Sense of an Ending* that, 'It is not that we are connoisseurs of chaos, but that we are surrounded by it, and equipped for coexistence with it only by our fictive powers.' To my mind, not to believe in invention, in our fictive powers, to believe that all is traceable, that the rabbit must finally be in the hole waiting is (because it's dead wrong) a certain recipe for the williwaws of disappointment, and a small but needless reproach to mankind's saving capacity to imagine what could be better and, with good hope then, to seek it. □

NOTES ON CONTRIBUTORS

Simon Armitage has published five volumes of poetry. 'Northern Soul' will appear in his recently completed book of prose, *All Points North*, to be published by Penguin.

Richard Ford's novels include *The Sportswriter* and *Independence Day*, which won a Pulitzer Prize. His most recent collection of stories, *Women with Men*, (Harvill/Knopf) was published last year. 'Where Does Writing Come From?' will appear in a collection of essays edited by Will Blythe, to be published by Little, Brown.

Edward Hoagland's sixteenth book, *Earth's Eye*, is being published next spring. His most recent books have been *Balancing Acts* and *Heart's Desire*.

Alfred Lawrie lives in London. He is a documentary researcher and an assistant editor on the forthcoming third edition of the *Fontana Dictionary of Modern Thought*.

Tim Lott's first book, *The Scent of Dried Roses*, won the PEN/J.R. Ackerley Award for Autobiography. His first novel, *A Satire About Male Friendship*, will be published next summer by Viking. He lives in London.

Tim Parks is a writer and translator living in Italy. His most recent novel, *Europa*, was shortlisted for the 1997 Booker prize. 'Destiny' will be included in *Adultery and Other Diversions* to be published by Secker and Warburg.

Richard Lloyd Parry is the Tokyo correspondent of the *Independent*. He is the author of a guidebook to Japan, published by Cadogan Books.

Todd McEwen's previous novels are *Fisher's Hornpipe* and *McX*. His third novel, *Arithmetic*, is published by Jonathan Cape.

Sebastião Salgado's book on migrant working men, *Workers*, was published in 1993. A member of the Network agency, he is currently engaged in a project on population movements around the world. His photographic awards include the Centenary Medal Award and Honorary Fellowship of the Royal Photographic Society of Great Britain.

Nicholas Shakespeare's *The Dancer Upstairs* (Harvill/Doubleday) won the American Library Association Award for the best novel of 1997. He is completing a biography of Bruce Chatwin to be published jointly by Harvill and Jonathan Cape. He was one of *Granta*'s Best of Young British Novelists.

Dani Shapiro's memoir, *Slow Motion*, will be published by Random House in the United States, and Bloomsbury in Britain. She is the author of three novels and lives in New York.